PETROLHEADS IN SHEDS

UNIQUE KIWI CAR COLLECTIONS

PETROLHEADS IN SHEDS

UNIQUE KIWI CAR COLLECTIONS

Steve Holmes

HarperCollins*Publishers*

HarperCollins*Publishers*

First published 2012
HarperCollinsPublishers (New Zealand) Limited
PO Box 1, Auckland, 1140

HarperCollins*Publishers*
31 View Road, Glenfield, Auckland 0627, New Zealand
Level 13, 201 Elizabeth Street, Sydney, NSW 2000, Australia
A 53, Sector 57, Noida, UP, India
77–85 Fulham Palace Road, London W6 8JB, United Kingdom
2 Bloor Street East, 20th floor, Toronto, Ontario M4W 1A8, Canada
10 East 53rd Street, New York, NY 10022, USA

National Library of New Zealand Cataloguing-in-Publication Data
Holmes, Steve, 1971-
Petrolheads in sheds / Steve Holmes.
ISBN 978-1-86950-988-0
1. Automobiles—Collectors and collecting—New Zealand.
I. Title.
629.2220922—dc 23

ISBN: 978 1 86950 988 0

Publisher: Bill Honeybone
Design and typesetting by Macarn Design
Cover image by Steve Holmes
All internal photographs by Steve Holmes, except those on pages 82 and 159–63 (*NZV8* magazine); page 123 (Hayes family); page 164 [small] (Rush family); pages 177–8 and 179 [bottom left and right] (Martin Rudow); pages 179 [top left and right] and 181 (Tony Garmey). Background images courtesy of shutterstock.com.
Printed by Bookbuilders, China

CONTENTS

INTRODUCTION

Believe it or not, the idea for this book didn't actually come from the *The Kiwi Hot Rodder's Guide to Life,* which I wrote a couple of years ago for HarperCollins and which was released in late 2011. *The Kiwi Hot Rodder's Guide to Life* was a book about Kiwi hot rodders, and their garages and car and automobilia collections. Despite the concept of this book being similar to that on Kiwi hot rodders, the idea for the book actually came from my more recent *The Kiwi Ute Driver's Guide to Life.* When compiling that book, which features a huge array of utes of all shapes, sizes, years and varieties, I'd often get the heads-up on a suitable vehicle, check with the owner for permission, and arrive at their house expecting to find a single-car garage with a ute parked inside — only to be confronted with a large and/or interesting barn, housing all manner of fascinating machinery!

With this same scenario occurring several times over, I began to wonder if perhaps a book on Kiwi motoring enthusiasts and the automotive collections they'd managed to amass, through either careful planning or just simple hoarding, might have some potential. I knew it'd certainly be fun to compile.

This book features the collections of 28 Kiwi petrolheads, from the far north to the deep south of New Zealand, and even one Kiwi living abroad — running an automotive business in the United States. The collections include vintage cars, classic cars, muscle cars, race cars and motorbikes. Although some collections are themed around one particular subject, many are multi-layered and venture well beyond. While the motorcar and motorbike are the predominant subjects, I was also amazed to find on my journeys, among other gems, a Tiger Moth, a Harvard, a traction engine and a Bren gun carrier, all tucked away casually in people's garages in a not too dissimilar way to how the average person might store their Toyota Corolla.

Garages are wonderful places. They're like living beings, a direct extension of their owner's personality. Some are tidy, others messy; some grand, others modest. They serve a purpose: they're a place of work and where work gets done. They're full of character, yet are constantly changing.

This book was an absolute joy to put together. I met some amazing people, many of whom I'll continue to remain in contact with. It never ceases to amaze me how many interesting, characterful and colourful collections are scattered around this tiny country of ours. And I really only scratched the surface!

BRENDAN

Brendan's collection may not be the largest in this book, but boy, is it full of quality! Brendan is a true muscle car enthusiast, and has owned an impressive list of road and race muscle cars over the years. Brendan has raced a brace of different Camaros, all of which have been second-generation models, kicking off with a red 1970 followed by one of those originally raced by Art McKee in the early 1970s in New Zealand production racing events. His current weapon of choice really is just that, a weapon. It is the car that was built for Wayne Anderson for Super GT racing back in the mid-1990s to beat up on all the late-model turbo-charged Porsches — which it did to great effect. Forward propulsion is provided by a behemoth all-alloy Donovan big-block V8. As well as racing his own cars, Brendan has also teamed up with another enthusiast featured in this book, Torana collector John, when the pair tackled Targa New Zealand in one of John's race cars.

At the time of my visit, Brendan also has a selection of really interesting road-going muscle cars. The beautiful green 1968 Camaro is a very rare Z/28 option model, and one of an even smaller number produced in this colour. The car itself has had a colourful past, having done a bit of circuit racing in the United States, judging by the plaques attached to the centre console. When Brendan purchased it in the mid-1990s, there was clear evidence that it had been thrashed pretty regularly during the 1970s and '80s in illegal street racing in Los Angeles. Of all the cars that have come and gone in Brendan's life, this is one that will remain with him, come what may.

Parked up next to the '68 Camaro is a 1966 Corvette roadster. Again, this is a special beast, being a genuine big-block 427 cubic inch, 425 horsepower car. This car has been in New Zealand for most of its life. Its former and longtime owner had it repainted in its current shade of blue, the same as all the other cars in his collection. The 'Vette is so original that Brendan is slightly embarrassed by the state of the engine bay — but to my mind this only makes it more interesting. This old Chevy just oozes character. A nice touch is the old 'carless days' sticker still inside the windscreen, a remnant of a hugely unpopular Muldoon government ruling from 1979 when, in response to the oil shocks of the time, owners of petrol vehicles weighing less than 2000 kg had to designate one day of the week on which their car wouldn't be driven. According to the sticker, this Corvette had to stay in the garage on

BFGoodrich
Radial T/A
Z/28
RARE Z

Brendan's beautiful 1969
Mustang Mach I Cobra Jet.

Wednesdays. Another snippet of this car's history is the small sticker still attached to the shifter console showing that it attended the 1978 National Rod Run in Palmerston North.

Brendan also owns a very rare 1969 Ford Mustang Mach I Cobra Jet, with its 428 cubic inch big-block motor. This was a car created by Ford specifically for drag racing. And the combination is terrifying. So purposefully is this car designed for just one single task, that it's fitted with four-wheel drum brakes! This is not a car designed to go around corners, nor stop in a hurry. This particular example is in amazing condition, even fitted with a factory oil-cooler, and Brendan has managed to track down a set of correct Firestone bias-ply tyres, which must make any wet-weather driving of this animal quite an adventure.

Brendan hinted that he might consider selling the Camaro race car at some stage down the track, but he is a racer and if that goes, something just as interesting will certainly take its place. Oh, and it'll almost certainly have eight cylinders!

HAINES HUNTER SS725
Nautech Electronics
MASON
Ray White

Brendan's other 1969 Mustang is this stunning award-winning Mach 1.

4A
PPROVED
EPAIRER
VW BEETLE
AA
EO 5471
AVWNUT

BRENT

I know straight up that it's pointless asking Brent how many Volkswagens he has owned over the years — I know that even he won't have a clue. Brent's love of Volkswagens, and in particular the air-cooled examples, is a fairly typical case of a hobby metamorphosing into a business. What began as a passion for building, restoring and modifying VWs for himself and a small number of fellow enthusiasts has long since outgrown its innocent beginnings and spawned into a full-time business. Brent not only buys and sells these chattering little German machines, but he also does everything from basic tuning and chassis work through to turnkey cars.

'I love doing what I do,' Brent tells me, 'but it's not a hobby any more, and I don't enjoy working on my own cars like I did before this became a business. Back when I worked for someone else, I'd go straight into the garage each night after work, often not even bothering to change out of my work clothes.' One thing Brent is very careful to do these days is to separate work life from home life. While his workshop is stuffed to breaking point with cars, parts, photos, model cars and every other VW-related piece of paraphernalia imaginable, at home there is barely a trace of his love for this marque.

When I visit, Brent immediately points me towards a very neat and tidy one-owner 1963 Volkswagen Variant (nicknamed 'Mr Badger' by its original owner). The last time I was here, his collection had been quite different. I clearly recall seeing a beautiful Beetle convertible and a rusty Karmann Ghia (both since sold) and that wasn't too many months ago, so there is clearly a strong demand for his services and the cars he sells. But the Variant is a keeper; unlike most of the vehicles Brent has, it's not for sale. It has done 500,000 km and spent its entire life in Stokes Valley, Lower Hutt. Brent knew the original owner, now deceased, for many years. Also here is the stunning VW truck which appeared in another of my books, *The Kiwi Ute Driver's Guide to Life*, plus a couple of Kombis and an assortment of Beetles of all ages. In the yard out back are a collection of 'parts cars' which Brent has picked up during his travels.

People's fascination with the air-cooled VW, the car initially bankrolled by Adolf Hitler and designed by Ferdinand Porsche, has always been strong, and fairly unique. So hardy are these machines, and so adaptable, that they've become the basis for everything from beach buggies to sports cars. For years, the VW

Kombi has been the vehicle of choice for cash-strapped Kiwis and Aussies making their way around Europe; although, with the value of these vehicles surging as they have done in recent years, this may become a thing of the past. Oh, by the way — for anyone wanting to relive the Kombi-based European adventures of their youth, Brent has two of them.

TOW-AWAY
NO
PARKING
GENUINE
SPARE PARTS
LOOK
AND ADMIRE
BUT PLEASE
DON'T TOUCH

RATBUS

MCB 1401(Blue)
DUB CITY

XN1170

CM 5697

IJ7376

Brian's incredible steam-powered 1924 Doble. When new, this vehicle commanded a price tag equivalent to three Rolls-Royces.

BRIAN

To try to categorize Brian simply doesn't do justice to the man himself, nor to his vast array of interests and skills. He is a car enthusiast, a motorbike enthusiast, an aeroplane enthusiast, a hot air balloon enthusiast and a steam enthusiast. His collection includes everything from a Tiger Moth to an impressive selection of cars, a steam boat and a traction engine. He has his pilot's licence, and has owned his 1942 Tiger Moth since 1979. Brian is also a hot air balloon pilot. As an engineer, he has a fascination with anything mechanical, and loves the challenge and complications presented by vintage vehicles, especially those a little out of the ordinary. What's more, he has kept most of what he has collected over the years.

So let's start at the beginning. When he was 14, Brian wanted to buy a motorbike but his mother wouldn't let him. She did, however, allow him to build a motor scooter — which he did, from scratch, and into which he squeezed a 350 cc Royal Enfield motor. Brian still owns this scooter. His first car was a 1927 Chrysler four-seat coupé. He still owns it. Furthermore, when the Chrysler was brand-new, it sat in a Nelson showroom next to a Chrysler four-passenger roadster (with the rumble seat); Brian now also owns the roadster. The Chrysler was getting on in years and worth little when he decided to replace it with a 1939 Dodge D11, hence his reasoning for keeping it. He still owns the Dodge. Brian's late wife, Loretta, was as much an enthusiast as Brian himself, and bought him a traction engine for his twenty-first birthday! Of course, he still owns the traction engine.

Perhaps Brian's most interesting vehicle is his 1924 Doble E-type steam car. This was the ultimate in steam cars and, when new, sported a price tag equivalent to three Rolls-Royces. Only 11 E-type Dobles are known to exist today, so Brian is part of an exclusive club which includes American chat-show host Jay Leno, who owns two examples. In fact, Brian drove one of Jay's Dobles when visiting his collection in Los Angeles. When running, the Doble is completely silent. It really doesn't make any noise. I'd heard from another enthusiast that one of Brian's party tricks is to drive up behind someone he knows at an event, and touch the back of their legs with the Doble's front bumper. Brian confirmed this to be true. 'Also,' he told me, 'it has a steam whistle just behind the front bumper, but you have to be a bit careful they don't have a bad heart!' Brian bought his Doble, which has been in New Zealand all

its life, in 1967 and had it up and running four years later — for 20 years, this was the only working Doble in the world. Brian's fascination with steam power also saw him import a steam paddleboat from the UK some years ago.

Brian certainly appears to have a love for the alternative directions in which vehicle manufacturers were heading in those early days. History shows that the internal combustion engine is what we came to rely on for nearly 100 years, but as well as steam power there were manufacturers who felt that electric power was the way to go. Brian owns a huge 1918 Detroit Electric, which is in remarkably original condition, and high on his list of priorities is to have it running again soon. 'I'd love to use this to tootle around town with,' he says. Currently, his 'town car' is an electric-powered 1997 Chevy S-10 pick-up.

Also in Brian's collection is a 1936 Cord 810, which he purchased in 1964, and a magnificent 1929 Bentley 6½ Litre, featuring a very early replica Le Mans Sports Tourer body with 'S'-stamped engine, suggesting the motor had been later updated to Speed Six specs. He also owns a 1902 French-built Mathieu, which he is currently restoring, and which is the only surviving Mathieu known to be in existence. This car has been in New Zealand since new. Brian is aiming to have it ready for the 2014 London to Brighton Veteran Car Run, which is open only to vehicles built up until 1904. The Mathieu engine and some other parts of the vehicle have been stamped with *Made in Paris* badges. Brian thinks the cars were initially designed/built in Paris, then moved to Belgium for further production when the Paris factory closed — possibly due to flooding from the Seine. He said they were made in the same factory where the Belgian Delins were produced. There is also an impressive 1927 Stutz, with a straight-eight motor, a 1925 Studebaker Special Six, a 1912 Wolseley, a 1904 Oldsmobile, a 1910 Flanders, and numerous motorbikes, including a 1912 Triumph, a water-cooled 1929 Scott, and a rotary-engined DKW. The oldest car in his collection is a steam-powered 1899 Locomobile. Squeezed in among everything are a couple of Isetta bubble cars from the 1950s and a 1964 BMW 700. 'That's for sale,' Brian told me. 'It's too modern for me.'

During my visit, Brian talks about trying to purchase a Stanley Steamer out of the United States. He shows me photos of the interior, which is littered with dials, knobs and gauges, not dissimilar to those of a steam train, which the driver constantly adjusts and tweaks. I can see such a challenge would be right up Brian's street.

Kellogg's
ALL-BRAN
AJAX

Brian's Mathieu, photographed circa 1902.

CHRIS

Those who have an interest in hot rodding will immediately recognize at least one of the cars in Chris's collection — his wild, primer-grey Willys coupé. The Willys, in coupé form, was built between 1937 and '42, and is right up there with the 1932 Ford coupé and roadster as far as hot rod porn goes. Chris's example is not only a New Zealand-new car — it also has some early Allcomer saloon car racing history, being powered by a Zephyr 6 motor and driven by Barry Pointon. It's also thought to have been raced by Red Dawson, before Dawson took on his more famous green Chevy V8-powered version. It was while sanding back some of the layers of paint that Chris found the Willys had previously been painted bright orange with a large number 37 on the door.

Chris bought the Willys as a body shell in rough condition, kept it for years, then set about fitting it with floors and getting it back on a chassis. He has built it as a gasser drag-style car, with straight axle and nose-up stance, and as a lookalike of the car that starred in the 1979 television movie *Hot Rod*. And like that car, it's powered by a big Chrysler Hemi that's spilling out of the space where the tiny four-cylinder Willys motor once sat.

The Willys coupé is just one of several Willys vehicles Chris owns. His others are all four-door models, and one of these is being rebuilt to replicate the paint scheme and mechanicals of the Pointon car, although it'll remain in four-door guise.

Chris runs a workshop specializing in metal fabrication and mechanical work and, as well as his Willys collection, he has several customer cars on the go, including a chopped Chevy pick-up and a Holden ute. The latter, rather than being fully modified, is getting more of a retro treatment.

Back at home, and Chris's collection continues. His daily driver is a fantastic-looking 1935 Plymouth two-door sedan, which, during his ownership, has amassed over 200,000 miles! The Plymouth is equipped with a towbar, and hauled the Willys coupé to the Hot Rod Blowout event in Auckland recently. Chris's back paddock and sheds are full of more cars and parts, including a neat-looking vintage speedway Modified, his self-built dragster pick-up, and a chopped Ford Popular body, which was an old hot rod from the 1970s.

Chris grew up around hot rods. His folks and grandparents were all involved and now he's a dad, his kids are into it as well. Despite popular belief, not all teenagers are fixated by Subaru WRXs and Mitsi Evos. Maybe the future is in good hands after all.

Frosty Jack
SIMONIZ

WILLYS
Operation
and Care

ROUTE
66
Coke
Coca-Cola
Coca-Cola
QUIK CPA

CLIVE

What can I say about Clive's garages, bar and car collection? It is simply *amazing*. It's really more like a tiny village from 50 years ago, and has the feel of having been transformed — lock, stock and barrel — from 1955 right *plonk* into Clive's back yard. When I arrive, Clive greets me with a big handshake and a bigger grin. Straight away, I already know two things about Clive: (1) he is incredibly passionate about his hobby, and his enthusiasm is quite contagious; and (2) he has a *very* fertile imagination, and the motivation and 'cajones' to follow through on the various ideas that come to him in the middle of the night when he should be asleep.

The first thing I notice when pulling up is what looks for all the world like the frontage of an early service station, in front of which is parked a very original-looking 1932 Ford five-window coupé. The second thing I notice is the front bodywork and wheels of a Mack truck parked nearby; it's been restored, but appears to have been converted for some other means. I quickly discover that the Mack is actually a mobile barbecue! Did I not say this guy has a fertile imagination?

Clive's main vehicle building was once base camp for his trucking firm. Now, where big rigs used to sit, there is a collection of beautiful 1930s Ford coupés, including a 1933 three-window, a '36 five-window and a '39 Deluxe. The '36 was a recent US import, and one which has already clocked up plenty of mileage visiting Beach Hop and Americarna. Both the '33 and the '39 are early New Zealand residents. The building where the old Fords are parked has been fully decked out to represent an early garage. Next door is where Clive keeps some of his larger-scale vintage vehicles, including an old fire engine. Next door to this Clive has built a blacksmith's shop, partly just for the hell of it and partly because he's amassed a large collection of old blacksmith's tools. He's even built a small settler-style hut, inside which are displayed early household utensils and appliances; again, just for the hell of it.

On the other side of the service station Clive has built a bar, which has been designed to replicate a 1950s American diner. Inside it's packed with retro furniture, a bar, jukebox, Coke machine (which spits out beer), and everything else you'd expect to have found in a diner in the 1950s. Even the music chiming from the stereo is period-correct!

Budweiser
Budweiser
Budweiser
Budweiser
Coca-Cola
INDIANA
43943A
TEXAS
BZX-59K
3TQD502
VDF 188
D35-066
Mack

But wait, there's more. We head down to Clive's trucking firm premises, where he and son Darren have their own workshop, and where a couple more early Ford projects are being undertaken. Darren is himself a petrolhead, and his crazy fenderless 1939 Ford Deluxe coupé dirt-track car is stored here. The company smoko room is packed with car magazines, pictures and model cars, while the office and reception area further display this family's love of all vehicles big and small, with a huge cabinet full of yet more model cars.

Clive isn't showing any signs of slowing down, and I am certain that the next time I return there will be evidence of his next magnificent creation; the idea for which will have come to him in the middle of the night.

Adjustable bench, originally out of the Petone Ford assembly plant.

26
WELLINGTON
DUNLOP
BP
SHELL

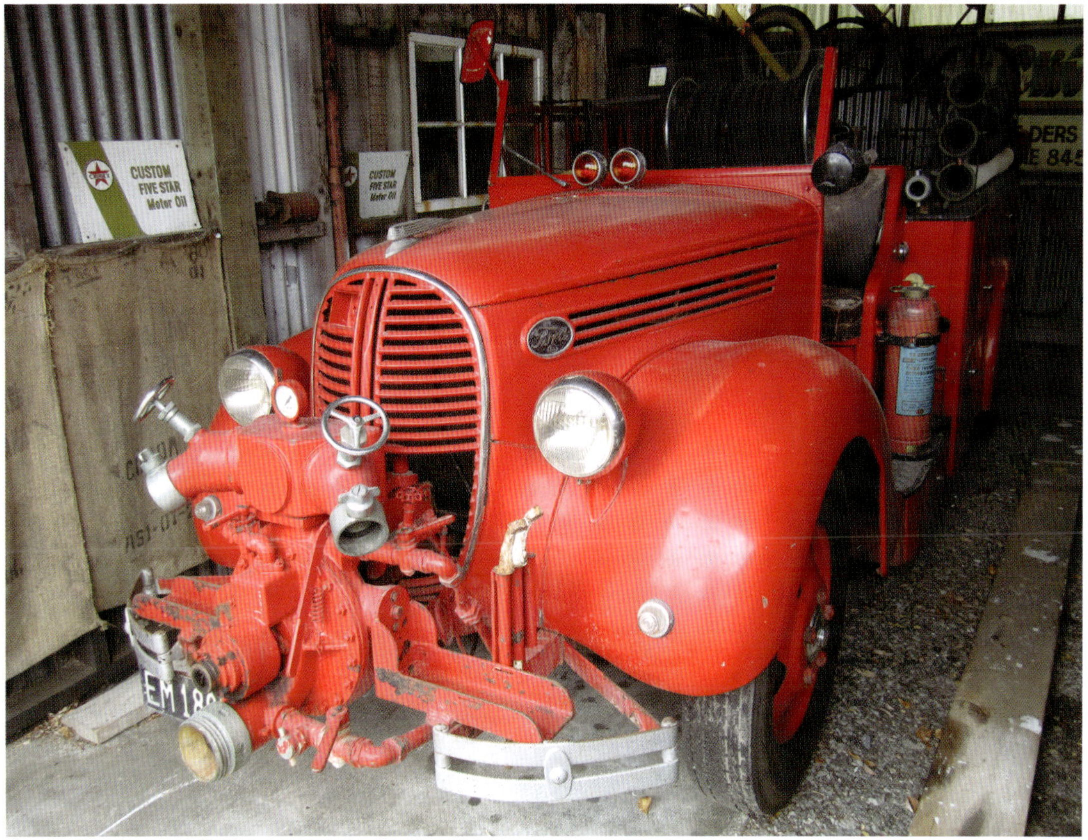
CUSTOM
FIVE STAR
Motor Oil

YE OLDE
Blacksmith

ANCHOR

"HOT DOG"
Mack
MACK

Ford
CLIVE TAYLOR
LIMITED.
CARTAGE CONTRACTOR
PARAPARAUMU

Bud
BURGERS
BEACH HOP
TEXACO
TEXACO
MOTOR OIL

Amount Purchased
8D
£1
BEER
Coca-Cola
Budweiser
Coca-Cola

199-982
HISTORIC
ROUTE
66
1932
Junkyard
Fashion Show
ICE COLD
Coca-Cola
MAGNUM
ELVIS
PRESLEY
DRINK
Coca-Cola
Coca-Cola
6 FOR 25¢

Coca-Cola
Coca-Cola
Coca-Cola
Amount Purchased
Coca-Cola
Coca-Cola 6 for 25¢

Norton
CVV 460

It doesn't seem to matter how much time I allow myself when I visit Horopito Motors, it's never enough. The last time I came here I made the fatal error of bringing my partner Helen with me. Big mistake! I was allocated 45 minutes and she followed me throughout, providing an ongoing commentary of how much time I had left. This time, I allowed a couple of hours. And it *still* wasn't enough.

Horopito Motors is unique for New Zealand. Sure, many of the cars that have been here for a long time are slowly retreating back into the earth from which they originally came. But hey, this ain't the Arizona desert; the Kiwi climate, for the most part, is not kind to metal. But the cars that sit in the grounds have, in many cases, had their trim and other important components removed for safekeeping. For anyone restoring a car built prior to 1980 that was available new in New Zealand, there is a good chance Horopito Motors will have parts for it, in good condition, stored safely indoors. There are several outbuildings that house masses of spare parts and a number of vehicles.

Horopito Motors has provided the backdrop for numerous movies, documentaries and music videos. Kiwi musician Rob Vegas recently filmed a music video here. The New Zealand cult film *Goodbye Pork Pie* used it for a scene as well. But Horopito Motors is best known for the 1982 Roger Donaldson flick *Smash Palace*, starring Bruno Lawrence. In fact, so synonymous with the Donaldson movie was Horopito Motors that pretty well any Kiwi car enthusiast will know what you're talking about if you tell them you're off to visit 'Smash Palace'.

Horopito Motors hasn't been standing still. They now have an area largely populated by cars from the 1960s through to the '90s, while the main buildings themselves have had a fantastic-looking makeover, to represent a Western-style town. Bill Cole established the company in the 1940s as a garage and motor repair shop. It was based out of a sawmill. Bill milled surrounding trees to form several of the buildings on the land, and the family home; the sawmill still stands on the property today. As cars came to the yard for dismantling Bill removed the parts he needed and the remains were kept on site, rather than being crushed. Over time, the collection of cars in the yard grew increasingly large to eventually cover several acres. Bill passed away in 1987, but his daughter Barbara and her husband Colin continue to run the business as Bill intended.

Y-ACETONE
ELDING
E HERE
FOSTER'S
LAGER

CE 662

Wandering around the acres of dead cars, it's incredible to see such a good chunk of New Zealand motoring history on display. The cars that were once common on our roads all sit here quietly rusting, and that is one of the attractions of this place. It's an amazing experience to just wander through and see what's there. Once upon a time there were numerous wrecker's yards dotted around New Zealand, much like Horopito Motors, but they've virtually all gone. This place is unique, and fascinating. The next time you're charging along SH1 south of Taupo, consider taking a detour inland, and make a visit. But just make sure the person you're dragging along with you actually wants to be there too. You'll enjoy it much more that way!

Ford

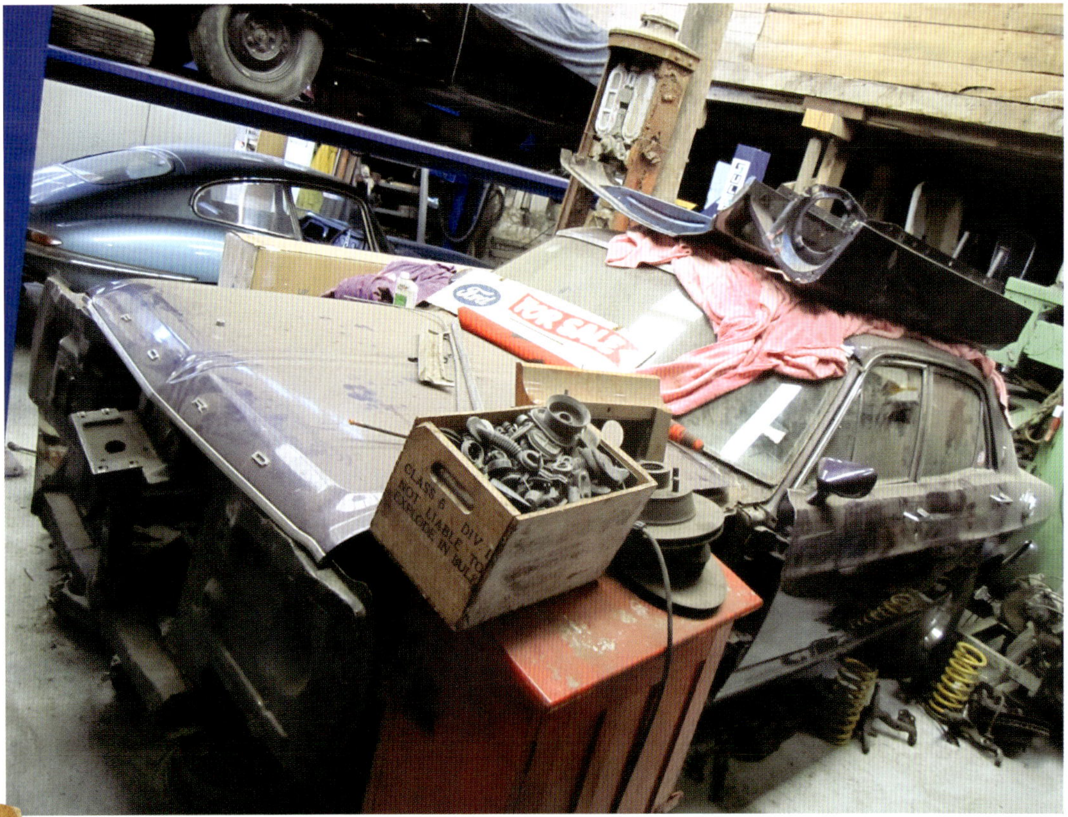
FOR SALE

FORD

BIG TREE
Frosty Jack
ICE CREAM
BIG TREE

24 HOUR
SERVICE
0800 28

DES

I first heard of Des through another member of the Vintage Car Club, who'd suggested Des would make a great addition to this book. Des is a fascinating character who has been collecting and restoring cars all his life. What I find refreshing is that many of the vehicles in his collection have been owned by Des for at least 30 years, some many more. He views cars, no matter how valuable or rare, as things to be driven and enjoyed, not mollycoddled and treated like china dolls. His cars are driven regularly, regardless of the weather; he is an active Vintage Car Club member and enjoys nothing more than giving his cars a good blast on an open road. He has even loaned his cars to other VCC members for car club rallies.

On meeting Des, he takes me through to the very clean and tidy four-car garage attached to his home, in which is housed, first up, a 1930 Graham-Paige, which he purchased back in 1963 and has since fully restored. Parked next to it is a pair of Austin 8s, one of which is a beautiful Australian-bodied roadster. He has owned the roadster since 1971. Out back is another garage, and inside is a magnificent 1958 Jaguar XK150, which Des bought in 1975 from a local car dealer. The Jag was, at the time, pretty tired and showing signs of possibly having had a competition life at some stage — along with the accompanying bodywork and chassis damage. A restoration was undertaken on the Jag in 2008, returning it to its current resplendent state. I note a plastic oil bottle behind the flowing Jaguar grille which looks slightly out of place. It's being used as a radiator overflow tank and is held in place by an old belt. 'Oh, that belt is off some fancy outfit my wife had. It's quite a fancy buckle, isn't it?' I love this combination of old-school practicality mixed with exotic late-1950s Jaguar styling. It shows this car is built to be used.

Recently sold from the collection is the 1963 Plymouth Belvedere Des's father purchased when new. Before Des bought the car in 1987 it had clocked up over 100,000 miles, and Des added a further 120,000 before finally selling it to another enthusiast who had been pestering him to sell it.

We then jump into another of Des's cars, a MkI Jaguar, and head out of town to where he has another collection of cars in a large pole barn; he's restoring these currently. In among this group are a 1924 Buick 4, a 1957 Jaguar Mark VIII, a Ford Model T, 1929 DeSoto (the first model year), and a pair of 1931 Grahams, one of which was originally purchased back in 1965 to provide spares for the Graham-Paige in his garage at home. A retired farmer, this is where Des

AO 9299

spends much of his time, restoring and rebuilding his cars. ‘People tell me at my age I shouldn’t be mucking around with these old cars — I should be taking things easy,’ says Des. ‘Well, that’s just ridiculous. My reply: You do what makes you happy, mate — and what’s the alternative? You only live once. Staying busy doing what you love keeps your mind sharp.’

CH 6999

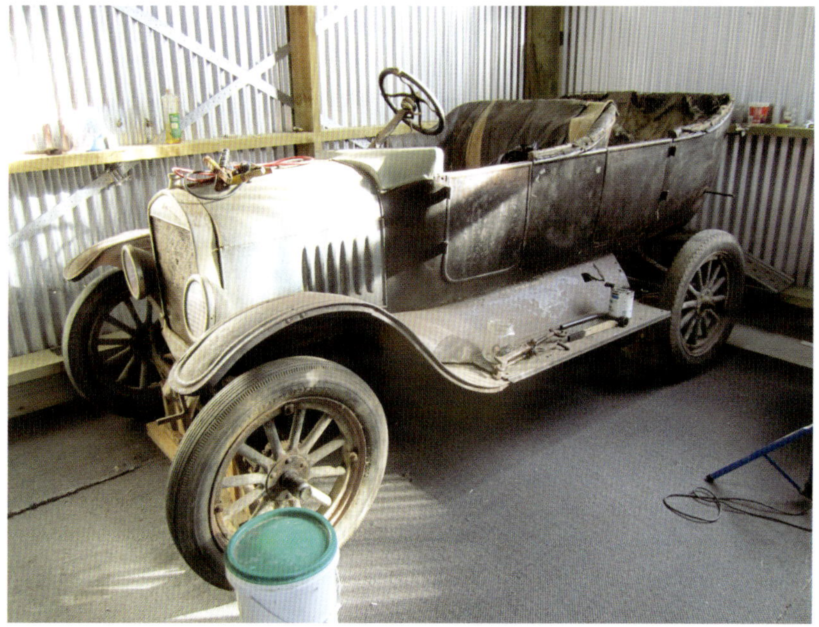

BONANZA
OTORCYCLE
EXPO
ATURDAY
23RD
MARCH
FEATURING WORLD
RECORD ATTEMPT
MOTORCYCLE
HILL CLIMB
SAT. 17th + SUN. 18th MARCH
TE WHARAU RD.
Gladstone
WELDWELL
44TQO
26USC
RSV

DOUG

At 60 years young, Doug has already lived the type of life most of us say we'd like to lead but ultimately chicken out of. A lifelong motorbike and motorbike-racing enthusiast, Doug has done it all, and is still going strong with some exciting plans for the future.

Doug purchased his first motorbike at the age of 14, a G80 Matchless 500. And, judging by his workshop and outbuildings, it's one of the few items he *hasn't* kept! Doug is a hoarder, and his collection is fascinating.

Doug has been racing motorbikes all his life. He's done it all, from solo speedway racing to hillclimbs with vintage sidecars, and he even holds the world grass track 1 mile record, which he claimed in 2002 riding a custom-built Triumph Spartan 750. But it was in 1988 when he took the ultimate plunge and purchased a brand-new Ducati 850 Superbike, one of only 200 built, and raced the bike at the Isle of Man TT.

Doug isn't a rich man. In fact, far from it. But he is determined. He didn't have any means to transport the Ducati from Italy, where he picked it up, to Calais to catch the ferry to England, so had a couple of German friends drive from Germany to collect him and then take him to France. It must have made for quite a sight as he pushed his brand-new, unridden racing Ducati onto the ferry!

After he'd competed in the Isle of Man TT, Doug spent much of the next two years in England, working a day job and racing the Ducati as much as his budget would allow. And he competed on some legendary tracks and in some legendary events, including the insane Ulster Grand Prix, a high-speed race through the Irish countryside between historic stone walls and with absolutely no margin for error. He also raced at Monza in Italy; Circuit Paul Ricard in France; Assen in the Netherlands; and in British events at places like Knockhill, Pembrey, Aberdeen Park, Scarborough, Donington, Snetterton, Oulton Park, Aintree and Elvington. After his visa ran out he headed back to New Zealand, but returned again as soon as he could muster the funds, and went on to race in the Isle of Man TT again. He raced in the TT in 1998, riding a Yamaha Thundercat 600, and again in 1999 on a Honda CBR600.

Among Doug's amazing collection, his Ducati has pride of place. He has also managed to assemble an eclectic collection of cars — although not through any obvious planning. These include a 1946 Ford coupé, which he purchased in the late '60s and which has sat quietly ever since the Flathead V8 quit in the early '70s.

139
139
DUCATI
Superbike
888
Doug
139
Greytown Plumbing LTD
Possibly the best semi passive cash flow franchise on the planet!
Greytown
RACING TEAM
BUTCHERY

750
SPARTAN
70

ONSHIP
onda Motorcycles L.M.V.D.
RECORD ATTEMPT

ONE MILE
Grasstrack
CHAMPIONSHIP
Sat. 19th APRIL
Greytown Racing Team
Motorcycles L.M.V.D.
BONANZA
MOTORCYCLE EXPO
SATURDAY 23RD MARCH
FEATURING WORLD RECORD ATTEMPT
MOTORCYCLE HILL CLIMB

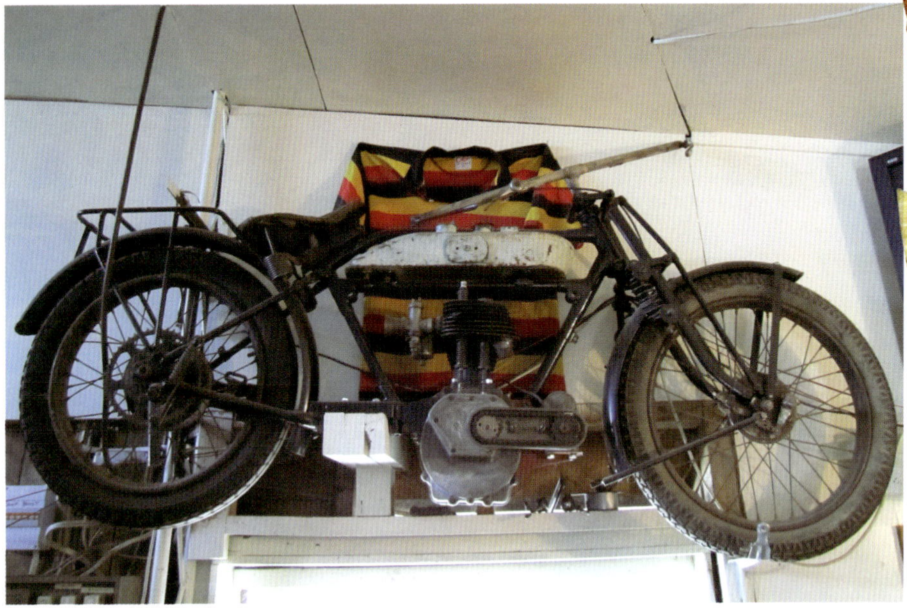

BONANZA
MOTORCYCLE
EXPO
SATURDAY
23RD
MARCH
FEATURING WORLD
RECORD ATTEMPT
Honda Motorcycles
Norton

FRANCIS

GET YOU HOME
AA
APPOINTED GARAGE
ASSOCIATION
DUNLOP
PLUME
Motor Spirit
Laurel
SOLARC
LOOK OUT!
GARAGE APPROVED BY MINISTER OF TRANSPORT
WARRANTS of FITNESS
SUPREME
DANGER
REPAIRS
CARS &
TRUCKS
GIRLING
ANDERSONS
LIMITED

SUPERCHARGED
SUPER SHELL
Ford
YP2891

Francis is the owner and creator of the Pointon Collection, on the outskirts of Masterton. This collection gives a fascinating insight into the history of New Zealand motoring with a very strong Wairarapa connection, as many of the cars and automotive pieces are from this part of the country.

Francis has been tinkering with vintage cars all his life. When he was 17, he went to work on a huge farming station on the Wairarapa coast, one of the first stations established in New Zealand. By the time Francis arrived the place was littered with fragments of its past, which included a massive collection of vintage cars — most of which remained in the exact place where they'd last been parked. The station was so big and so isolated that it had its own blacksmith.

Francis found a 1927 Chevy that had long since been discarded. He turned it back into a runner, and used it as his transportation while on the station. Eventually, he left to take up employment at Fagan Motors, a long-running Wairarapa Ford and Mazda dealership. Francis left Fagan's in 1977 to start his own automotive business, and it was during a quiet spell two years later that he decided to purchase and restore a 1935 Vauxhall 14, which he still owns, and which was the starting point in his now very large collection.

Much of the Pointon Collection was purchased from old automotive dealerships that were either closing down or being refurbished, and much of it was picked up for a song, as Francis began collecting long before items like old tin signs and oil company products became fashionable with collectors.

The Pointon Collection officially became a museum in 1993, one year after Francis and his wife Gaye, a fellow enthusiast, bought a large wooden building that had been first built in Featherston and was used as a prisoner of war camp during World War One. The building was later pulled apart and shifted to Pahiatua, where it became a Polish refugee camp following World War Two.

Francis had never really intended to start his own museum; it's just that his collection grew to such a size people kept telling him this was something he should do with it. He says he's stopped buying cars and parts as the collection is now large enough — but then confessed to me on my visit that he had 20 or so vehicles on his Trade Me watchlist! Do collectors ever really stop collecting?

SHELL X100 MOTOR OIL
GREASE
SEALED
SHELL
MOTOR OIL

OK1935
1935
VAUXHALL

Lockheed
DELCO
ALEMITE

Castrol
mind how you cross
MOTORISTS
WHEN YOU DRIVE
HOLIDAY TRAFFIC
KEEP LEFT
KEEP LEFT

AA
MICHELIN
BIG TREE
64-597
173-468
90-353
77-304
Goodrich
MICHELIN
JOHN BULL TYRES
Mobiloil
Drive in for
FREE COMICS
FREE ROAD MAPS
TJ 602
HARLEY-DAVIDSON
PARK
Guaranteed
Pure
BIG TREE
Motor Spirit
FIRE
H2O

JMACAN

Powered by FORD
99
99
LAST RACE OF THE CENTUR

L41·936
L41·794
E32·755
438·505
BORON
PREMIER
REPCO
AMPOL
75YRS
SERVICE
TO THE
MOTORING
ACE
POINTN

gives up to
creamery butter
Fiat 127
BB V8

LT 1530
BD 5573
CH 7987
AQ 104
AP 161
AQ 104
CG 2821
BD 5573
LT 1530
CJ 4325
AH 4044
IM 3925
ES 7196
CN 2828
CJ 6641

POINTON FAMILY
GARAGE
FILL UP WITH
SHELL
OIL AND SPIRIT

TYRES AND RETREADS

GM DEALER TEAM
CMB

GARRY

I've known Garry for years. He is essentially a classic car dealer, buying and selling classic and vintage cars. But unlike most dealers, Garry doesn't actively sell his cars. Most are in fact purchased and enjoyed, and are only considered for resale if he needs space or feels the need to move on to something else. Some he keeps for years; some he may never sell. But all this makes Garry's collection even more interesting, as I rarely know what it is he is going to have when I visit. Furthermore, Garry's tastes are quite varied, and his collection is thus quite eclectic.

Before my latest visit I knew about at least three of Garry's cars because he has owned them for a while. These cars are kept in the first garage we view. One is his very special Holden VH Commodore SS. This is one of just 30 built by General Motors New Zealand to compete in the Benson & Hedges endurance racing series in the early 1980s. GMNZ basically took advantage of a loophole in the rules that allowed them to produce a very limited number of 'homologation specials', designed specifically for the B&H series. Kiwi motoring journalist Robin Curtis, who ran the GMNZ competition department at the time, was largely responsible for these cars, and Robin had Australian racing legend Peter Brock supply many of the parts that went into them, along with Brock's own knowledge on converting them to race-winners. At the time of their release, the Kiwi SS Commodores were the fastest Commodores available anywhere, being devoid of the power-sapping catalytic converters their Aussie cousins were fitted with.

Twenty-nine of the SS Commodores were painted white with red and blue stripes; the remaining one became a lone black car with gold stripes, built for GMNZ sales manager Loring Lyons and dubbed 'Black BeSS'. Garry actually owned this car back in the late 1980s. He now owns one of the 29 white cars, this being one of the two GM Dealer Team race cars, which was driven by Peter Brock and David Oxton. The second GM Dealer Team car was driven by Denny Hulme and Peter Janson. Incidentally, this car is now owned by Garry's son Mike, and is parked next to Garry's Brock/Oxton car when I visit.

Also among Garry's collection is a beautifully restored Holden Torana XU-1, this particular car having once been raced by Jim Richards. Garry bought the Torana many years ago in poor shape, and had it completely restored. Parked next to the Torana is another car with interesting competition history: the Team JPS BMW 325i raced in the Australian Touring Car Championship by Tony Longhurst in the mid-1980s. There are also motorbikes in Garry's collection, along with Jason McEwen's helmet and leathers from his Britten racing days.

Outside, but undercover, is a an original-looking Austin A40, while a Sunbeam Tiger lives in the garage next to the house. From here, another garage reveals once more the varied nature of Garry's collection. As he swings open the door, I'm struck by the quite unrelated but still really interesting combination of a Ford Thunderbird, an ex-works Lada rally car, a BDA Escort rally car, an Austin 7 commercial, and a Tatra! I did say Garry's tastes were eclectic. The walls of this garage are lined with hundreds of old New Zealand motorsport photos, which makes for just about the most interesting way to wallpaper a garage you can get.

Tiger

A7 VAN

CEH594
A7 VAN

ANNUAL MOTOR CAR RACES

Classic Cars

GEOFF

I was once told that Geoff's incredible collection of Holdens is the largest privately owned Holden fleet in New Zealand outside that of the New Zealand Police. While I don't know how true this is because I don't know what other collections might be locked away, I also don't know whether the New Zealand Police actually *own* their cars or just lease them. Either way, Geoff's Holden collection is *large*! It includes a vast number of models, ranging from the oldest, a Holden FJ, right through to the newest, a VE Commodore. Exactly how many Holdens Geoff owns, I don't think even he knows.

'If I could get a VX and a VY Commodore,' Geoff tells me, 'I'd then have at least one example of every model Commodore made, from the first VB through to the newest VE.' You'd think tracking down either model of Commodore would be a fairly straightforward process, but Geoff is quite particular about what he purchases and, where possible, he gravitates towards low-ownership, low-mileage cars. He even has a very rare (mainly due to the lukewarm response from the public when new) four-cylinder Commodore.

What I find so interesting about Geoff's Holden collection is that he has opted for the bread-and-butter models, the Mum and Dad cars, rather than the high-end stuff. The cars he has in his collection are what were common on New Zealand roads for decades, cars we simply took for granted. And yet these are now the hardest models to find, because they weren't preserved as carefully as the more desirable, more expensive models, like the Monaros and the Brock Commodores. And so Geoff's collection makes for a fascinating walk through time, through our own motoring history of the cars we grew up with.

Geoff is currently rebuilding a Holden HJ ute which he bought in 2011. This vehicle was fitted with a factory 253 cubic inch V8. Amazingly, it's the first V8 car Geoff has owned! Since purchasing this ute the V8 bug has obviously taken hold, as Geoff has spent much of the past year building a very accurate Holden HQ SS replica, complete with its own 253ci V8.

Geoff has been a Holden enthusiast all his life, basically. Before his collection began, he raced in the once wildly popular HQ Holden series before moving on to the Commodore Cup. He still owns both the cars he raced then. Geoff was included in another book I wrote, *The Kiwi Ute Driver's Guide to Life*, in which his Holden FE ute was featured. Since that visit his collection has grown further, and he proudly points out a superb-looking and highly original HQ station wagon,

HJ8372

ND9585
MY58FE
ROBERTSON HOLDEN

a rare Australian-assembled model with electric rear window, bucket seats and manual gearbox.

Geoff likes his cars to look factory-original, and goes to great lengths to return them to this state. Most had been at least slightly modified over the years by the time he got hold of them, but Geoff has gone to every effort to bring them back to factory standard, right down to fitting them with factory wheels and hubcaps.

HOLDEN
51
GEOFF HILL
51
www.hqmotorsport.co.nz
Firestone
51
Cummins
51
Cummins

The famous ex-Jim Richards Sidchrome Mustang, which George has owned for many years and which he is in the process of restoring.

GEORGE

When I got the green light to go ahead with this book, one of the first people I contacted was George because his collection combines two of my great loves: muscle cars and motorsport. At first George agreed, but a few weeks later he contacted me to say he felt it best to decline the offer. George is owner of the famous New Zealand tin-top saloon racer, the Sidchrome Mustang, since buying the car off Jerry Clayton at the tender age of 21, in the late 1970s. He raced it for several years on a tight budget, but retired it in the mid-1980s. George has been so busy lately giving the Mustang a huge restoration to return it to the track that some of his garage space has become too messy for his own high standards, and he didn't want it photographed this way. I didn't want to accept this, so eventually George and I came to an agreement: I'd photograph the tidy areas of his garage, and the rest of the photos would be supplied by *NZV8* magazine from a feature they'd compiled on George recently.

George's muscle car collection is impressive; as are his garages, which are set up in a horseshoe-style layout. There is more than enough garage space for most people, though not for George. When I visited, his collection included the Sidchrome Mustang, a genuine XC Falcon Cobra, a 427 cubic inch Mercury Comet, a Z28 Camaro, a GTHO Falcon and the Robbie Francevic/John Morton *Metro* magazine-sponsored Group A Falcon, along with a Plymouth 'Cuda, a '69 Camaro, a '74 Super Duty Pontiac Firebird, a De Tomaso Pantera, a '69 Boss Mustang and a '65 Mustang fastback, the Grant Sylvester TraNZam Mustang, a 1970 Ford Torino 'Twister Special', and a Mercury Cyclone Spoiler II (Cale Yarborough Special) fitted with a Boss 429 — plus several others. The '69 Camaro is set to become a Yenko tribute car, while the Twister Special is one of just four known four-speed examples left in the world! The 'Cuda will be fitted with a 426 cubic inch Hemi; most of George's cars have either been, or are due to be, race-prepared.

As well as the cars, George has amassed a serious collection of parts, including engine, transmission, diff, suspension, wheels, tyres … the list goes on. In among it all is an amazing collection of desirable inlet manifolds and carburettors, some of which are incredibly rare.

His collection has been built up as a result of plenty of hard work, with the GTHO a good example of how he grafted to get what he wanted. He was

Rare Group A XE Falcon, originally raced by Robbie Francevic/John Morton.

17 at the time and on a wage of $25 per week as an apprentice electrician — the repayment on the GTHO was $20 per week. So George spent his evenings and weekends doing callout work until the car was paid for. In all the years he's been racing he's had little sponsor support, so has learnt to rebuild his own engines, do all his own mechanical work and welding, and almost every other task required to keep his cars running.

When I visit George he is well down the route of restoring the famous Sidchrome Mustang in which Jim Richards won the 1974 New Zealand Saloon Car Championship. This is the car that helped launch Richards' career in Australia when he took it with him (with young family in tow) in 1975 to take on the Aussies on their home soil. When Richards was finished with the Mustang it was sent back to New Zealand and owner Jerry Clayton began preparations to sell it. George spotted it in a workshop and approached Clayton about buying it, eventually stringing together a deal that saw him trade another car, use his savings and borrow the rest from a work colleague. But he got his dream car, and has owned it ever since.

It amazes me that in this tiny country of ours collections like this exist, and it's a credit to enthusiasts like George who make it happen.

Castrol

26
RACING OIL

WEST AUCKLAND
ENGINE RECONDITIONERS
20
427cu.in
Crystal PANEL & PAINT
AMBER ELECTRICAL
holman moody

76
AUTOMOTIVE

GRANT

Though a young bloke, Grant has packed an awful lot of living into a short number of years. After training as a mechanic in Gore, he soon left New Zealand to work for an IMSA racing team in the United States. In time, Grant became a gun for hire, offering his race-engineering services as a freelancer to rally teams all around the world. His talents were quickly pounced on by several teams, and he found himself living a high-speed, jet-set lifestyle in which he was constantly on the go, commuting back and forth from the UK to Europe and the US.

Eventually, the constant commuting took its toll. Grant ended up exhausted, and gave up the fast-paced motorsport life to return to New Zealand. But despite his best intentions, he was soon back again in the northern hemisphere, working as an engineer for a rally team in the UK. When this team disbanded, Grant and another member bought the team out and set up their own company. They got picked up by SEAT, the Spanish motor vehicle brand which was heavily involved in touring-car racing, in both the World Touring Car Championship and several domestic championships. Grant's team was to become the SEAT factory team in the British Touring Car Championship, and they also ran the one-make SEAT Cupra Championship, which involved running and maintaining 24 identical cars.

As the recent recession hit and car manufacturers began to withdraw from motorsport involvement, SEAT pulled the pin on its BTCC efforts, and Grant returned once more to New Zealand, this time with his wife Julie. Here he set up his own company offering an array of services from race preparation and trackside support to fabrication and restoration.

Interestingly, despite a career at the very pointy end of the motorsport spectrum, Grant himself claims to have never actually raced a modern car. Despite carving out a living building and preparing race cars, he also loves to climb into the driving seat — but when he does, it's behind the wheel of an historic race car.

Grant's collection has been assembled from cars bought in New Zealand and overseas. Whereas many historic race cars seem to leave our shores as their values rise, Grant has actually been responsible for bringing cars *into* New Zealand. Perhaps the jewel in the crown is his incredible

HISTORIC RACE SERIES
31
Masters
HSCC
SUNOCO

Castrol
MT POKAKA
TECH
DILUSI
Keith Andrews
TRUCKS
FUSO

Keith
Holley

1952 Connaught A5. This car, built from new with a four-cylinder Lea-Francis motor, made its racing debut in the 1953 British Grand Prix at Silverstone, driven by Leslie Marr. The Connaught raced throughout Britain over the next three years before making its way to South Africa, and was eventually purchased by Kiwi Ron Duncan in 1957 and imported into New Zealand. The Connaught ended up with Jim Fenton, who raced it until 1959 before having it cloaked with a sports-car body. When he eventually retired the Connaught in 1961, he kept it for several decades until it was purchased by Grant.

Other cars in Grant's collection include a McLaren M10 Formula 5000, a pair of Brabham BT16s, one of which was raced by Denny Hulme, a Cooper, and the New Zealand specials: the Capella and the Begg Twin Cam. Grant also purchased, while in the UK, a MkII Zephyr that had been a race car there since the early 1970s, plus a Lotus Cortina which he was part-way through race-preparing for British and European historic touring-car racing when he returned to New Zealand.

Unfortunately for Grant, a cracked vertebra has kept him out of the driver's seat for the last couple of years, but he is recovering well and expects to get back behind the wheel soon.

HSL
305

Extremely rare 1952 Connaught A5, one of the few genuine F1 cars to come to New Zealand and remain here.

JEREMY

I first met Jeremy at the launch of my previous book, *The Kiwi Hot Rodder's Guide to Life*. Jeremy began telling me about his infatuation with the long since deceased American vehicle manufacturer Willys-Overland Motors. Probably best known as the creators of the Jeep, Willys was at one stage the second-largest vehicle manufacturer behind the Ford Motor Company, but spent much of its existence flirting with bankruptcy until it created the Jeep just prior to World War Two.

Prior to the war, Willys had come to be a manufacturer of modestly priced vehicles. Following the war, it temporarily ceased production of its passenger vehicles while it concentrated on seeking out a post-war market for the Jeep. Willys eventually re-entered the passenger car market in 1952 but never recovered market share, and the company was eventually bought out by Kaiser Motors and renamed Kaiser-Jeep. The American Motor Corporation purchased Kaiser-Jeep in 1970, with the struggling AMC eventually being bought by Chrysler in the 1980s. Of all the cars made by Willys, the ones best known today, other than the Jeep, are the dramatic aero-style cars built from 1937 up until the United States entered the war. Jeremy has owned one of these models since 1977.

Although we met at the launch of a hot rodding book, Jeremy's interests lie in originality. He bought his 1937 Willys four-door, complete with its little four-banger motor, and used it as his daily transport for nine years. Since then, he has also owned a couple more Willys vehicles and still has his 1935 example, which originally arrived in New Zealand in 1936 as a left-hand drive car.

After arriving at Jeremy's house we enter his garage, which is decorated along all the trusses with hundreds of old New Zealand licence plates. He used to own a fairly significant collection of tin signs, but has since sold these on. Entering the garage, there is the '37 Willys — but I'm surprised to see, parked next to it, a hot rod! However, as Jeremy explains, this car was built as a hot rod in the United States in the 1950s or '60s and so is quite an historic car just the way it is. It's a steel-bodied Model A Roadster pick-up on a Model A frame, imported into New Zealand a couple of years ago. It was fitted with a Chrysler Hemi, but this has been sold separately, along with its wheels. Jeremy has been busy rebuilding it, including fitting a small-block Chevy and much chassis work to make it safe, useable and legal so that he can use it for summer cruising.

As interesting as Jeremy's cars are, I notice on the roof of his '35 Willys several sections of miniature railway track, and ask what these are for. Before I know it we're heading towards another building, inside which is a massive and quite impressive collection of 1:20,3 scale model railway trains and carriages, plus spare track and associated appendages. This shed also houses a pair of cabinets, inside which are several model cars and a large collection of books; however, my curiosity has me pushing to find out more about the railway. Jeremy then leads me out behind his house into a large area where he has created a hugely impressive outdoor model railway, with everything from villages to hills, tunnels and bridges — and all built (except for the houses) by Jeremy! It's definitely one of the coolest things I've seen, and it was completely unexpected.

REMO

SHELL
KEROSINE

JIM

It was Jeremy (see page 93) who suggested that Jim would make a good addition to the book. 'He owns a bunch of stuff; old petrol station pumps, tin signs, a Bren gun carrier,' Jeremy casually explained. *A Bren gun carrier?* I just had to see this.

Jim has what he describes as some sort of family illness, one that requires him to collect stuff — any stuff, but especially interesting, historical stuff — and then hoard it. Apparently, other members of his family have possessed the same 'collector' gene. Jim owns a quite massive, sprawling and ever-growing collection that includes not just vehicles, but virtually anything historical. His family has a long and significant history with the Taranaki region, owning farmland that has remained in the family for generations. Jim's great-grandfather was James Livingston, an important figure in the Taranaki area. James was one of the first people in Taranaki to own a motorcar. His first was a steam car, and the family still owns the steering wheel and column from it. James's second car was a 1906 Darracq, which was purchased new, and this car has remained in the family throughout its life. Jim is a regular attendee of Vintage Car Club events with the Darracq.

To his credit, Jim is trying to bring his massive collection together under one roof. He has commissioned a large barn to be built on the family property, where everything will be housed together. This should have been completed months prior to my visit, had there not been a series of hold-ups with the architect which delayed the project. And so, Jim's collection is currently spread among several buildings, over two farms!

In another garage is the infamous 1943 Bren gun carrier I'd been told about. Jim actually purchased this particular example back in 1977, after it had spent many years in a farmer's paddock, slowly disappearing under a boxthorn bush. The Bren gun carrier is currently undergoing another rebuild, including a new paint job and refurbishment of its Ford flathead V8 motor. In yet another shed sits a 1927 Jordan, which Jim bought in 1978, next to which is parked his son's sinister-looking 1955 Nash.

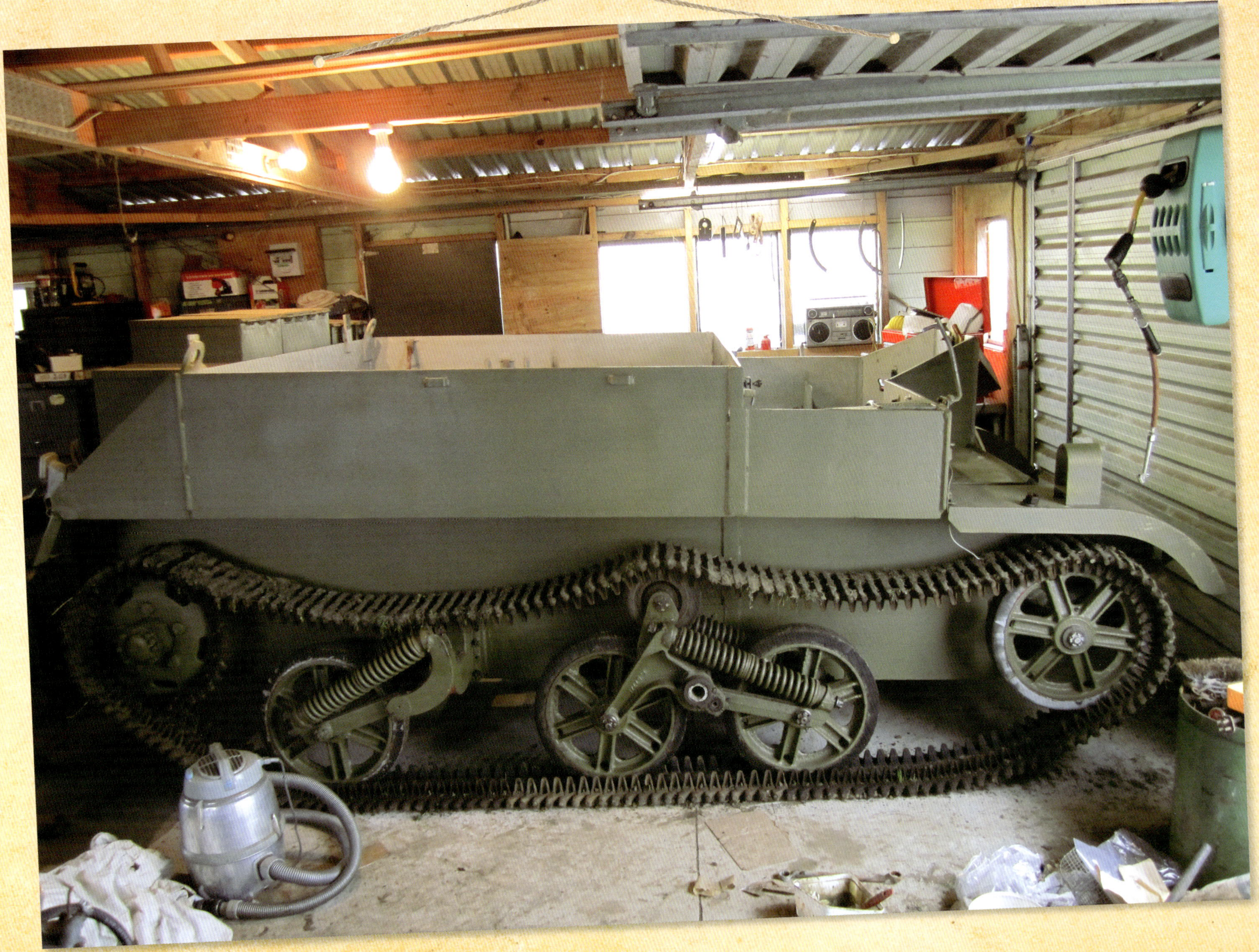

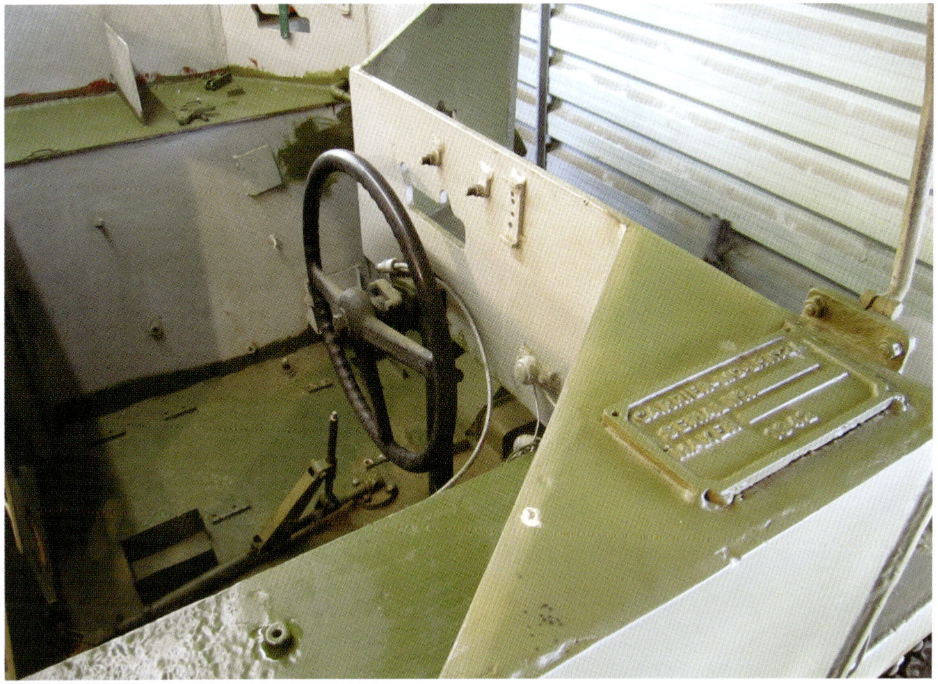

Ford flathead V8, soon to be reunited with Jim's Bren gun carrier.

Jim isn't fixated only with mechanical things; he's also purchased two local historic buildings that were otherwise due for demolition. One of these houses holds mountains of items relating to his family over the generations, including everything from metal Fun-Ho! toys, to hand grenades, to his uncle's old photographic equipment.

Once we've finished going through the huge collection at their house, I follow Jim 20 minutes down the road to the family farm, where yet more sheds hide old vehicles and an impressive array of tin signs, petrol pumps and other historic Kiwi motoring items. Interestingly, the Patea Tourist Trophy, held from 1948, took place just up the road from the family farm.

Jim's new barn can't come soon enough. It'll be amazing to see this entire collection under one roof. But I get the feeling, as I'm sure Jim does too, that no matter how big the barn is, it'll eventually get outgrown.

CHECK YOUR
QUICK ACTING
COOPER'S
DIPPING
POWDER
WARNING
PROTECTED BY
SECURITAS
GUARANTEED LIFE
AUTOMATIC CORRECT-LEVEL TOPPING UP
Gidday . . .
I'm Vince Martin and this is a
DUNLOP
STOCKIST
DUNLOP
Reidrubber
CORRECT INFLATION
MEANS LONGER TYRE LIFE
MOTORWAYS
Firestone
CARRY A SPARE
Power-Full

CAUTION
ONE CAR
BRIDGE
SCHOOLBUS
7.45-8.15A.M.

HOLDEN
134
ARP
DUNLOP

JOHN

Without wanting to state the blindingly obvious, John is a Torana enthusiast. Quite how he became such a Torana enthusiast is something even *he* can't explain, as his first love was Minis. But the Torana obsession has well and truly taken hold. John bought his first Torana when he was 18, selling it again a few years later. He tracked this car down a few years ago and purchased it back, but has since sold it again. His collection now includes an impressive list of Bathurst specials, including an August 1971-released Bathurst LC XU-1 in 'Lina Mint' green, one of just 299 built; a 1972 LJ XU-1 in 'Strike Me Pink' and a 1972 LJ XU-1 Bathurst special in 'The Lone O Ranger' orange; an August 1973-released LJ XU-1 Bathurst special in 'Tangerine', one of 150 built; and a 1973 LJ XU-1 in 'Orchid Met' metallic paint.

The pair of later-model Toranas in the collection are third-generation L34s, both in 'Barbados Green'. One of these John imported from Australia, requiring a rebuild, but he then found another car in New Zealand and the Aussie car remains incomplete. One way a genuine L34 can be identified over a replica is in the very rough way in which the standard wheel arches have been cut out to allow for wide racing wheels, which are covered by the fibreglass bolt-on flares. Harry Firth, who was team manager at the Holden Dealer Team and who created the L34, cut the arches with tin snips! The replicas are always far more cleanly cut.

Among the collection John has a pair of active race cars, these being the genuine XU-1 in 'The Lone O Ranger' orange and a more recent acquisition, a yellow GTR. John had bought the 'Strike Me Pink' XU-1 as a race car, and he and good mate, Brendan (see page 8), raced it in the Targa New Zealand. At the time, it was painted yellow, but when John learned that it was a rare 'Strike Me Pink' car he retired it from racing and had it restored to its correct colour. Only 15 XU-1s were built in this colour, the bright pink not being a terribly masculine choice in the very heterosexual era of the early 1970s!

John's current weapon of choice for motor racing is the yellow GTR. When I visit, this is being stripped for a rebuild, having had each of its corners knocked off in a recent on-track incident. The car features a rare alloy Duggan head and dry-sump and produces 340 hp — a pretty impressive figure for one of these motors.

As well as the Torana collection John also has a pair of Mini Coopers, one of which is a race car fitted with an Ardun head. A Lotus Escort also has a

place in among all the Holdens. The building in which John keeps all his cars is an old showroom which was relocated to this spot many years ago, and it makes for quite a sight when you first drive up, given that it's out the back of John's house. It really is like arriving at a car dealer's showroom — in 1974! John has his own workshop where he does all his own engine work on everything except the yellow race car, which he outsources. And as you'd expect, given that this is a collection built over a lifetime, he has amassed an impressive collection of spare parts.

CELLAR

GTR
XU-1

GTR XU-1

KERRY

'The reason we had the shed built this tall was so we could mount the Harvard up on poles,' Kerry explains casually as he unlocks the door to his giant garage. His announcement was so matter of fact that I almost didn't comprehend what he'd just said. But, as the door opened, there it was — a bright-yellow Harvard, stored along the back wall behind an eclectic assortment of everything Kerry and his father Cliff have amassed over the years. The collection includes everything from Holden Toranas to go-karts to veteran cars to vintage bulldozers. It's quite something to take in. So I start with the one subject in the collection I do actually have a little knowledge on: the Toranas.

Kerry is something of a Torana fan. He owns three examples, each with its own unique identity and purpose. The red one, he explains, is an A9X replica. This is his 'hot rod', and it gets used regularly. His reason for having this car is really due to the significance of the other two Toranas. The 'Chamois' example is a genuine A9X four-door, and the only A9X to be fitted with the combination of 'Chamois' paint and a tan interior. Not a lot of people realize that Holden built the A9X as both two- and four-door models, as the two-door was by far the most popular choice for race teams, for which the A9X was created. But Kerry prefers the look of the four-door, and finds it a little more user-friendly. This is an extremely rare car.

The third Torana, the 'Lina Mint' green example, is also something quite special. Apart from being a genuine XU-1, Kerry discovered — almost by accident — that this is the very car raced during the early 1970s in both the Castrol GTX Production P/Car Championship and in various endurance races by celebrated single-seater and saloon-car racer Jim Palmer, entered by Ebbett Motors. It was while away travelling with his family that Kerry's son found a picture of the car in Tim Chadwick's book *Saloon Car Racing in New Zealand: The Classic Years*, and noticed that the number plate matched the car at home!

The shed has a number of vintage bulldozers stored in it, some of which were purchased by Kerry's father Cliff, along with the beautiful International bus Cliff started his business in, working as a mobile engineer. Then the Harvard. Again, this was one of Cliff's purchases. He'd actually bought it around 1962, along with another Harvard, from a Government Stores tender

Horrell & Co.
A GRADE MOTOR
PRECISION & GENERAL
ENGINEERS
Horrell & Co.
SONY

— paying £95 for the pair! This wasn't Cliff's first aeroplane purchase, however. In 1957 he bought six Mosquitos, from which he removed the Rolls-Royce Merlin engines and scrapped the rest.

All throughout Kerry's barn are artefacts from his and his family's automotive and engineering history, right down to the tin-plate toys he had as a child. I only wish I'd been clever enough to have kept the toys I had as a child, rather than wrecking them.

ENGINEERS
CATERPILLAR
PHONE
267 M
HOLT

MADE IN CHINA
CTN NO

CATERPILLAR
648

Horrell & Co.
SLR 5000
SLRA9X

Horrell & Co.
SLRA9X

MAX

There are some impressive collections in this book, and what we have scattered around garages throughout New Zealand never ceases to amaze me. But in the case of Max, I reckon that he himself makes for an even more interesting story than does his impressive collection of cars.

Max, like a number of Kiwis, made his way to England in the 1960s to be part of the large motorsport industry over there. He'd learnt his trade back in New Zealand building and racing go-karts, followed by TQ Midget speedway cars. He built a rear-engined 500 cc BSA-powered speedway car which he named the MiniMax. This machine was the first speedway car in New Zealand to be fitted with four-wheel disc brakes, and it had a four-speed gearbox so that it could double as a hillclimb racer. In 1965, Max left for England with a few of his mates, selling the MiniMax to John Hollings who placed second two years running in the New Zealand Hillclimb Championship.

Once Max's ship arrived in England, he quickly picked up work with the Brabham racing team, building F3 cars. Wanting to branch out, he then took a job offer from an American racing driver, Cliff Howard, for whom he would crew at several European Formula 3 racing events over the following months. From there he crewed for Charlie Crichton-Stuart in the Stirling Moss Automobile Racing Team (SMART). Then, after a season as Jack Brabham's F2 mechanic, Max eventually ended up working for Ken Tyrrell, whose team was making the step up from Formula 2 to Formula 1 in 1968, running the French Matra chassis with Ford's DFV Cosworth V8. Max crewed for Jackie Stewart, who finished an impressive second in the World Driver's Championship in 1968 and then went one better the following year, winning the World title. This was the first of three World Championships for both Tyrrell and Stewart.

Max would become the subject of an Eoin Young article for the UK-based *Autosport* magazine, and was jointly awarded, with Jackie's other mechanic, Roger Hill, the British Racing Mechanics Club Ken Taylor Memorial Trophy for his efforts and successes. He'd well and truly arrived, and was now an integral part of the Tyrrell team and an established member of the Formula 1 community. But Max had reached the pinnacle of his career and wanted to try leading a normal life, so made the decision to return to New Zealand for good with his wife Christina. Following a season helping Derek Bell run a Brabham BT26 Cosworth during the 1970 Tasman Series, Max settled in to lead the kind of life most of us would consider normal, but which must have felt unbelievably quiet and sedate to him compared with the incredible fast-paced, jet-setting adventure he'd had previously.

28

In more recent years, just prior to and since retiring, Max has taken on several road and race car restoration projects, including a 1939 Austin Ruby, the 'Sherlock Holmes' V8-60-powered speedway Midget racer (which Max is part-owner of), and a 1929 Willys Whippet. In 2009, Max and friend Laurie purchased the remains of two of the five JBS 500 racing cars that were brought into New Zealand in the 1950s. One of these two cars was originally imported by Laurie's father while the other was brought in by Ron Frost, who built the Levin racing circuit and became president of Motorsport New Zealand. Out of interest, Max's Austin 7 has a plaque attached to the grille given to him by the great Juan Manuel Fangio — a reminder of the fulfilling life Max has led. Juan gave Max the plaque and a personally signed letter of thanks for being the mechanic on the winning car in the Argentine Temporada F3 series in early 1966.

37RUBY

ESC788

Burt Munro's 1920 Indian Scout
600cc side valve to 1000cc OHV.
The World's Fastest Indian
528MO
35

When I first speak with Neville about being featured in this book he quickly agrees, and then proceeds to provide me with a contact address for the collection, which also happens to be his place of work. When I question this, he tells me the collection is kept at work. The immediate image that comes to mind is of an outbuilding off from the main part of his business, in which his family's collection is stored. I couldn't have been more wrong.

E Hayes & Sons was founded by Ernest Hayes in 1895, as an engineering business in Central Otago. One of Ernest's sons, Irving, opened the first E Hayes & Sons store in Invercargill in 1934, on Leven Street. Eventually, his son Norman began working for the family business in 1942 — Norman being the father of Neville, who is now general manager of the business. In 1956, a further building was erected in Dee Street, which runs parallel to Leven Street, to house the increasing number of products E Hayes & Sons was selling; in 1974 the neighbouring Wrightcars building was purchased, into which the business expanded, with a further extension taking place six years later. In 2009, yet another adjoining building was purchased and developed into more retail space. E Hayes & Sons now fills an entire city block between Dee and Leven Streets. Although predominantly a Hammer Hardware outlet, E Hayes & Sons is essentially a department store, offering everything from tools to kitchenware.

I first became familiar with the name Burt Munro when I read George Begg and Clive A Lind's book *When the Engine Roars: The Motor Racing Life of George Begg*. (Norman Hayes is also featured and pictured in Begg's book, with the fully functioning engine he built from scrap parts to prove a point to a friend — that an internal combustion engine need only have the 'correct amount of air and petrol sucked into a cylinder, compressed and fired by a spark plug' to work, and that it need not be a dynamically tuned piece of precision engineering.) Begg, another Southland racer, became best known for the series of racing cars he built during the 1960s and '70s, but began his racing career on motorbikes.

Burt Munro became internationally famous, long after his death, through the brilliant Roger Donaldson film *The World's Fastest Indian* (in which Neville's son Jarn Hayes rode one of the bikes of the Southland rockers that appear early in the film). Although items relating to Munro are now highly prized, the Hayes family, and in particular the late Norman Hayes — a motorbike racer himself —

YAMAHA
650
8

Buy a Bosch Blue 18 V Striker II Combo & get
Coolerbox
BOSCH BLUE GOES AS HARD AS YOU DO
bosch-pt.com.au
BOSCH
Invented for life
Aerofast
MAXI FASTENERS
anzor
1941 Mark One Rotrax
speedway bike 500cc
J.A.P engine

appreciated the significant achievements of Munro long before he became a household name. Munro was born in Edendale, near Invercargill, and spent his entire life in the area; the Hayes family knew him well.

Munro was best known for his highly modified 1920 Indian Scout motorbike which he took to Bonneville on nine occasions, beginning in 1962. With this bike he'd eventually set class and world records, the last being a World Class S-A 1000 cc in 1967 with an average speed of 183.586 mph and a one-way speed of 190.07 mph. This record stands to this day, and is the fastest officially recorded speed for an Indian motorcycle.

Another of Munro's bikes was a 1936 MSS 500 cc Velocette, which he also modified heavily. He'd planned to take it to Bonneville, but failing health prevented this. After a partial stroke in 1977 and preferring that his bikes remain in Southland, Munro sold both the Indian (without its streamliner bodywork, which remained in the United States after his final Bonneville trip) and the Velocette to Norman and Neville Hayes. Both of these motorbikes, along with a replica of Munro's Bonneville streamliner bodywork, one of two made for *The World's Fastest Indian*, are on display at E Hayes & Sons, along with a staggering collection of other motorbikes, both road and racing. Most of these are owned by the Hayes family, having remained in the family most of their lives, while others are on loan from fellow enthusiasts.

The Hayes family's love of history spills over into other fascinating displays that include everything from an early E Hayes & Sons delivery vehicle, to the 'scrap' motor built by Norman and mentioned in Begg's book, to Neville's own collection of muscle cars, and even the first Begg racing car built, the Begg 650, which is on loan from another local enthusiast. Another great thing about the Hayes family collection is that it can be viewed any time the shop is open.

35

Burt Munro's old motorbike trailer is also part of the incredible Hayes collection.

SUZUKI
13

E. HAYES & SONS
LIMITED
ARDWARE

NICK

I'd been told some good things about Nick and his collection of cars and automobilia, but when I phone him to enquire if he'd be keen to appear in this book, it seems a little unlikely. On describing the book to Nick and asking if he'd like to be included, his reply is short and to the point: 'No, not really,' is all he says. 'OK, no problem,' I reply, 'it's not for everyone.' I am about to hang up when he says, 'I don't want my garage at home featured, but you can come to my workshop.' I figure that, this being a functioning workshop that caters to all types of vehicles, it'd have its limitations. 'Is your workshop quite interesting then?' I ask. 'Most people seem to think so,' he replies, 'but the next time you're passing by, come and take a look.'

And so, a couple of weeks later on my way home from visiting another garage, I take a detour to see Nick — and my fears that the balance between being a place of interest and a functioning workshop won't work prove completely unfounded. Yes, Nick's garage is a functioning workshop, but *wow*, it sure is interesting! Housed in a superb old building that was once a new car dealership, Nick's garage is like a living time warp that transports anyone who visits it back in time 50 years.

Nick has decked out the interior of the building with some of his large collection of vintage automobilia, and given the walls a two-tone coat of yellow and blue paint to further add to the 1950s period feel. When I first visit, there is a scattering of vintage cars and traditional hot rods parked in various places around the building. Some of these are part of the decor, some are customer cars, and some are either Nick's or his mates'. In among the old cars stand some modern cars; customer cars that are the bread and butter of Nick's business. Nick suggests I return on a weekend, so that he can move the customer cars outside and I can wander around taking photos without being disrupted. So that's what I do.

What Nick has managed to achieve here is impressive. This place is as much a functioning workshop as any in New Zealand, yet it has a character that is now long gone in most garages. There is a '57 Chevy pick-up, intended to be the shop truck but now sitting permanently in a staged yet fully functioning service bay. At the rear of the building is a Model A Ford, perched on a hoist, looking for all the world like a scene from the 1930s. Nick owns the famous Mike Gearing roadster, which has its own spot in the workshop. Scattered throughout the building are old oil company tin signs and other automobilia that bring the place to life, and give it real character.

Nick is a guy who just loves to collect, and he has built his garage — his everyday business — into something that has become a shrine for his love of history and the days of old. Why can't all workshops be this interesting?

Agip
motor oils
PENNZOIL
LODGE
TEXACO MOTOR SPIRIT
Mobiloil
DUNLOP
MARFAK
Lubrication
LUBRICATION
MOTOR SPIRIT
TEXACO
MOTOR SPIRIT
CHEVROLET
COOL57
ASK
FOR IT
CG 5597
ASK
FOR IT
STP

MACKIE'S GARAGE
Goodrich Tires
SAFETY GOLDEN PLY
Levi's
JEANSWEAR
BFGoodrich

Dunlop
have the tyre
that's right for you
ASK FOR IT
PENNZOIL
Mobiloil

BP

Mobil
HAVOLINE
MOTOR OIL
HEAVY MEDIUM
TEXACO

STOP

Mobiloil
INQUIRIES
VELLUMOID

Reidrubber

Protune
AUTOMOTIVE
PENNZOIL

BP

PLUME
SHELL
HEPOLITE Oilmaster
Engineered PISTON RINGS

WAKEFIELD
CASTRO
MOTOR OIL
BRITISH
LABOUR DAY, OCT. 23
WHIPPET RACING
SUPERCHARGED
SUPER SHELL
Firestone
95th Reunion
WELCOME
HOME
31·474
44

PETER

It is Tim Rush (see page 164) who recommends I visit Peter. Tim says that Peter has a motorbike museum at his home. Now different people have different opinions on what constitutes a museum, but Tim has a better idea than most, with his family running their own museum. But even so, I'm not at all prepared for Peter's collection.

Quite how someone comes to own such a vast and interesting collection always intrigues me. But once I get talking with Peter, I quickly begin to gain an appreciation for how this collection came about. Firstly, Peter's father Andy began collecting motorbikes in the late 1940s, and Peter continued the tradition. Secondly, Peter keeps virtually *everything* he buys and collects! Little wonder that this place is as impressive as it is.

After chatting for a few minutes about the book and what I'm hoping to achieve, Peter shows me through a couple of small outbuildings that have a selection of motorbikes and associated stored parts, as well as a shipping container full of more motorbikes. Then, finally, we get to the bit I'm most looking forward to. Swinging open the door to the huge barn Peter has in his front yard, I enter Peter's motorbike museum. Just when I think I've seen it all, here in front of me is a two-storeyed museum packed with amazing old (and old-ish) motorbikes, along with display cabinets full of models, memorabilia, automobilia and walls lined with yet more related items. 'We've got about 100 bikes in here, but I've actually got about 300 altogether,' Peter tells me. 'But these ones are the best.'

In among the collection are several stunning early American Harley Davidsons and Indians (including a 1904 Indian), along with early British bikes such as Triumph and Norton. What I love is that almost all are in original condition, which brings real character to the feel of the museum. Sitting in pride of place is an impressive and mammoth 1000 cc Militaire Car cycle-car, complete with drop-down trainer-type rear wheels. This bike has a reverse gear, and the extra wheels provide stability when it's reversing. There's a New Zealand-built Black Dart in among the collection and even a bizarre all-wheel drive Rokon, which was an all-terrain vehicle that predated the quad bike but failed to sell in large numbers due to its exorbitant price tag. Peter even has the leather pants Steve McQueen wore in the 1971 movie *On Any Sunday*. Another neat addition is Peter's own 'No Club. Lone Wolf' leather

jacket from his younger riding days, explaining his non-affiliation to any one club.

Besides the motorbike museum, Peter has also compiled an impressive collection of New Zealand motoring magazines, many of which he has had since a teenager in the 1960s. Some he picked up when an old service station was due for demolition; he removed them as nobody else appeared interested. They include *Wheeling* magazine, published from 1913 to 1921, and the *New Zealand Motor and Cycle Journal*, published from 1909 to 1934.

Peter's collection is a private museum, and is open by appointment only.

1904 INDIAN.
1904

TEXACO

THRILLS
DUNLOP

31·474

DUNLOP
RETREADS

ROKON

1912
Motosacoche
290c.c. side valve

Valvoline
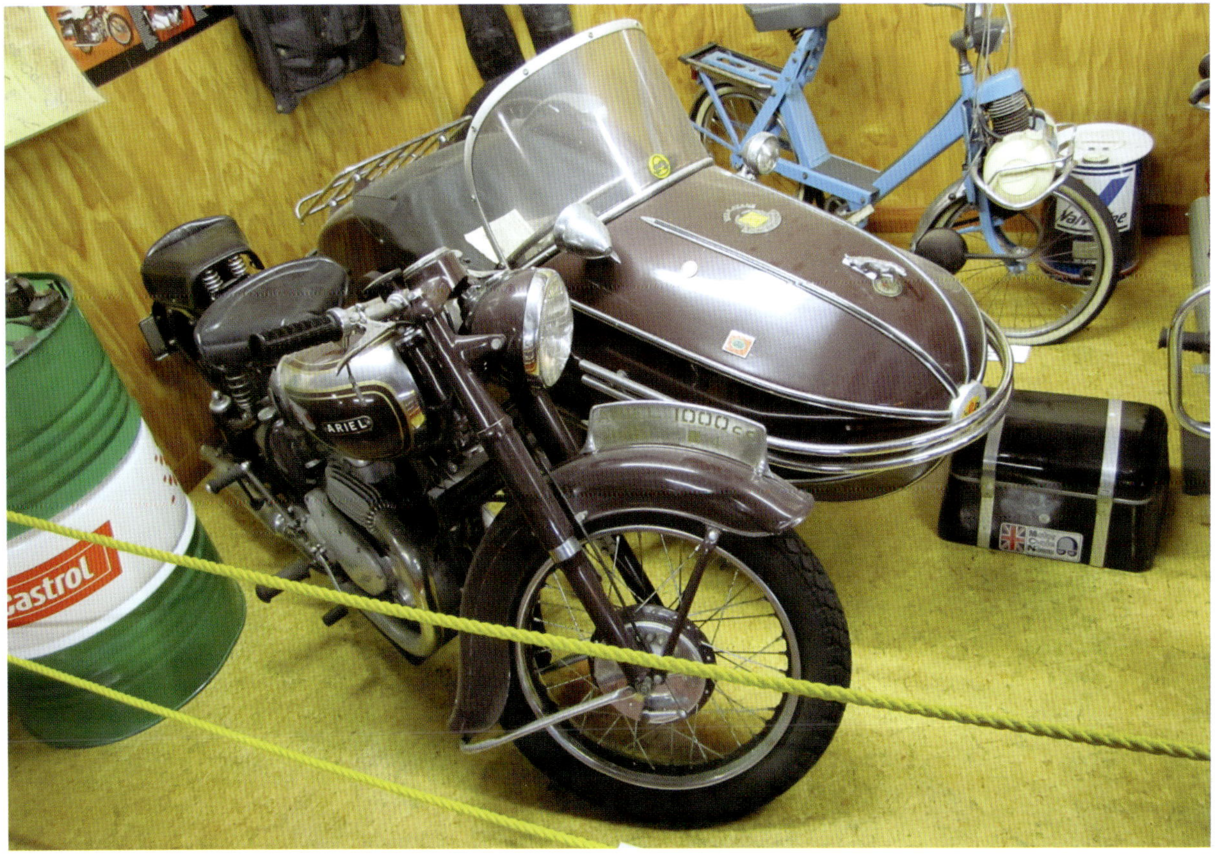
ARIEL

Mobiloil

motorcycle with
sidecar

15.453

RHYS

I'd first got to know Rhys through www.theroaringseason.com — the historic motorsport website and discussion forum I run. Rhys is a motor-racing enthusiast, and has been all his life. He started out in 1972 when he purchased one of the Skoda S110Ls that were sent out to New Zealand for that year's Heatway Rally. He campaigned this car for two years, entering 54 events, until deciding to retire from the sport due to the costs involved. From there he spent many years competing in land yacht racing.

Eventually, Rhys found his way back to his first love, car racing, and became involved with the Vintage Car Club of New Zealand. He is now one of those who enthusiastically support the Roycroft Trophy event for predominantly pre-1960 race cars and do what they can to support the cause. Rhys has owned a vast number of vehicles over the years, and tends to gravitate towards some real oddities — such as the Volcoupe, a curious little two-seater sports car fitted with a Volkswagen Beetle motor and with the wheelbase dimensions of a Cooper 500 race car, making it quite a tiny vehicle.

Rhys appears to have a love for French cars. In the driveway of his property on the day I visit is a Peugeot 404, built as a replica of the cars that competed in the East African Safari Rally, while behind his garage is a Peugeot 203. His main mode of transport is a Peugeot 306. The obvious imposter here is a Volvo 242, of a similar variety to those that were so popular in touring-car racing during the mid-1980s, and with which Robbie Francevic won the 1985 Wellington Street Race and the 1986 Australian Touring Car Championship. But it's inside his garage where the real rarities are kept.

As Rhys pulls up the garage door, the first thing I spot is the unmistakable French blue paint and curvaceous rear end of a Renault Alpine A110. This low-slung sports car is one of just five examples in New Zealand, and is a rare early two-headlight version. The A110 is a 1965 model, which Rhys bought in Mexico. There was a very small number of these cars actually built in Mexico, but Rhys has yet to learn whether this is one of these or a French import. Rhys also gets to ride shotgun in another Alpine, as co-driver for Donald Webster in Donald's competition A110, in which the pair have tackled Targa New Zealand for several years.

IMPERIAL AIRWAYS USE
SHELL PETROL EXCLUSIVELY
DRIVER
MECHANIC
1960 05 2010
50 YEARS PEUGEOT 404
OCTOBER 2010
RENAULT
KZ 307
VLB 545X
RENAULT
JZR
500
Biche

DRIVER
MECHANIC
1960 05 2010
50 YEARS PEUGEOT 404
DUNLOP TARGA TROPHY
DUNLOP
Targa
2nd
2nd IN CATEGORY
DUNLOP
Targa
NEW ZEALAND'S BIGGEST
MOTORSPORT EVENT
OCTOBER 2010
LABOUR DAY MONDAY 25TH OCTOBER > SATURDAY 30TH OCTOBER
AUCKLAND > NEW PLYMOUTH > PALMERSTON NORTH > WELLINGTON

New Zealand
Classic Car
FRENCH EVOLUTION
ALPINE
A110

Next to the A110 is a partially restored Buckler 90, the history of which Rhys has been trying to unravel. It is a very early English chassised car, possibly owned and raced by Kiwi car-builder Ferris de Joux. Rhys will eventually complete the Buckler's restoration and get it back out for road and historic race duties.

Also in the garage is a fantastic-looking cycle-car Rhys has been building as a mini replica of an ERA. This little machine is going to be a heap of fun when it's finished! Around the walls are remnants of Rhys's past, including photos of his land yachting days, plus a picture of the amazing Volcoupe. Rhys also owns a Ford 10 Special and an Austin 7 Special, both competition race machines he uses to blow off steam with the VCCNZ.

RICK

On a grey, wet and windy morning, I pull up outside Rick's building in downtown Invercargill. He is already outside, loading up a trailer that carries his son's kart and spares to race meetings. We shake hands and he leads me inside, where I'm struck by a long, long passageway completely chocker with race cars, spares and hordes of parts. Rick had given me a brief overview of what he has here during our phone conversation, but I still wasn't prepared for what I was seeing. The opening section to Rick's workshop is dedicated to karting, with several karts, race suits and related parts. Rick runs Mainland Karting South, and is the local agent for Monaco Karts.

Just glancing around, I can see the recently restored McBegg big-bore sports car owned by Wally Willmott, who was Bruce McLaren's first employee when he began his own racing team. Above the McBegg sits a BMW M3 race car, a Team BMW machine raced by the CiBiEmme team during 1987, while next to this pair is a beautiful Alfa and the BMW in which Tim Harvey won the 1992 British Touring Car Championship. A quick scour down the passageway reveals a Chevy Monte Carlo NASCAR stock car, one of the Tony Longhurst Racing Benson & Hedges BMW M3s and at least two more M3 race cars, plus various part-built cars, chassis, body panels and mountains of parts.

Talking to Rick, I can tell straight away that he knows his stuff. Most of the cars here are customer cars, most with owners in Australia and beyond. Rick specializes in restoring and race-preparing these cars. Some he runs for his customers — they simply fly in, helmet in hand, and Rick has their car at the track, ready to go — while others just want their car to be restored or race-prepared and take care of everything else themselves.

I wonder how it is that, way down here in Invercargill, Rick has managed to acquire so many international customers and be fortunate enough to have so many historic race cars in his shop. It turns out that he worked for Tony Longhurst back in the old Group A racing days in Australia, in the late 1980s and early '90s, when Longhurst was running BMW M3s. After returning to New Zealand Rick then did another stint in Australia, working for Peter Doulman, who also ran BMW M3s in the Australian Touring Car Championship. On returning to New Zealand again, Rick was eventually approached by an enthusiast wishing to purchase and race a BMW M3 in historic racing events, who wondered if Rick would mind looking over a car for him, then race-preparing it. From here, Rick's fleet of customer cars snowballed.

24
59
Brake Parts Cleaner
TONY KART

Rick's real speciality is with Group A cars, 'Group A' being the international touring-car regulations that were used throughout Britain and Europe, Japan, Australia and New Zealand during the latter half of the 1980s and the early 1990s. Rick has owned several Group A cars over the years, and has been one of the main instigators of the new 'Historic Touring Cars' category that provides a place for these cars to race throughout New Zealand. 'As well as the cars in here, there's another 18 in storage,' Rick tells me. I briefly wonder if he'll take me to see them, but I quickly realize that what he has here in his workshop is more than enough for one chapter!

As well as the McBegg and the Tim Harvey BTCC winner (which, incidentally, was one of the two cars used by team owner Vic Lee for drug smuggling, having its doors and other cavities packed with cocaine on several occasions between Europe and England), I find another big-bore sports car — this being the McLaren M12 Can-Am car originally imported into New Zealand by the Bruce McLaren Trust from Japan — plus the B&H BMW M3 in which Denny Hulme died at Bathurst in 1992. The M3 that won the 1988 Wellington Street Race is here, as is the Pukekohe round-winning Schnitzer M3 from the 1992 Wellington Street Race series, as well as Canadian Jay Esterer's McRae GM1 Formula 5000, which was being crated up, ready to be shipped back to Canada after its recent New Zealand tour.

It really is a completely unexpected pleasure for me to see so much history under one roof.

23
sport auto

HULME
MORRIS
26

BENSON & HEDGES RACING
20
BENSON & HEDGES
RACING
RECARO
TOOHEYS
YOKOHAMA

EXIDE
EXIDE

ESSO
8
BILSTEIN
QUBIE
HORIBA
DYMAG
CORBEAU
Shell Advanced Fuels
AUTOSPORT
23

220

44

GOODYEAR
5
McLAREN

STAN

The incredible Southward Car Museum in Paraparaumu is not just a world-class museum — it's a national treasure. For anyone who hasn't visited the museum lately, I can't recommend enough that you make the effort to get back there. It really is a special place. Although the museum first threw open its doors in 1979, Sir Len Southward began his collection in 1956 with the purchase of a Ford Model T. As the collection gathered momentum, it eventually outgrew the room it was housed in at Southward Tube Mills, and Len set about having the current purpose-built facility erected.

Sir Len Southward was a keen motoring and motorsport enthusiast all his life, winning the Masport Cup in 1948 aboard his mighty Allison V12 aero-engined speedboat *Redhead*, and becoming the first person in Australasia to exceed 100 mph on water. The Southward collection began following a trip to Britain during which both Len and wife Vera watched the finish of a veteran car run in Birmingham. The collection continues to grow, even today. Many of the cars, motorbikes and other artefacts were purchased during international trips; some at auctions, others by complete good fortune. What's so fascinating about the collection is that it's not based on any one theme; rather, just cars or motorbikes that Len himself took an interest in. It features some of the rarest, most desirable cars in the world, and some of the most modest. But each has a fascinating story to tell, and its inclusion in the Southward collection is often as interesting as its prior history.

When I set out to put this book together, I always wanted to include the Southward Car Museum. But I didn't want to include the museum itself. After all, this is a book about *garages*, about the private collections scattered around New Zealand that are generally not open to the public. But the Southward collection is not an exception. I wanted to get into the areas of the Southward collection that are not normally accessible. I knew that the museum has its own restoration buildings, I knew that a massive collection of spare parts has been amassed over the years, and I knew that there were cars which have been sitting quietly for decades, awaiting their turn for restoration and to be rolled into the public arena of the museum itself. This was where I wanted to be and, thanks to museum promotions manager Hayden Beissel who arranged permission from his grandfather Stan Bellamore, Sir Len's brother-in-law, I was privileged enough to be given access.

My tour begins in the restoration building where Hayden's uncle John and father Bernie are part of a small team of dedicated craftsmen who, at this time, are restoring a rare front-wheel drive V8 Cord. This building holds several

MERCER
ITALA

pieces of interesting old machinery, tools, tables and further automotive wonderment. We then pass through a door revealing shelves and shelves of engine parts for a multitude of makes and models. From there, we move to another storage area, in which thousands more spare parts can be found, including everything from mechanical to electrical parts. Then through another door and into a large room filled with crates upon crates, stacked carefully on top of each other, containing complete motors, motor parts, bodywork and an assortment of other items. There's everything in here, right down to a big V12 Lincoln-Zephyr engine block and gearbox. Hayden then points up at a crate on which is simply scribbled *Maserati 250*. Inside this crate are the spare parts that came with the museum's Maserati 250F which Len Southward purchased off Chris Amon's father, at the time when young Chris was about to set off for Europe to pursue a motor-racing career that would see him become a Le Mans winner and Ferrari works driver.

With my jaw now firmly on the ground, we exit this building and head across to another storage shed, this one housing approximately 40 cars awaiting attention. The first to greet me is a beautiful, aluminium-bodied Alvis. Beyond this are rows of rare and fascinating vehicles, including a curious Russian ZIM along with an assortment of Stutz, Cadillac and Packard, right through to a Skoda. Another car of interest is an early hybrid 1918 Owen Magnetic, which John hopes to soon get his teeth into restoring — as much for the challenge of getting it to run again as its links with modern-day fuel-conscious vehicles, despite the modern offerings being far less charismatic.

The cars in this part of the museum were publicly shown for the first time at the inaugural Southward Museum Open Day, which is set to become an annual event and is already massively popular. The Southward Car Museum is the largest privately owned car collection in the southern hemisphere, and something all car enthusiasts should embrace. All this started by a hard-working guy who began his career as a messenger boy for a motor importer in Wellington.

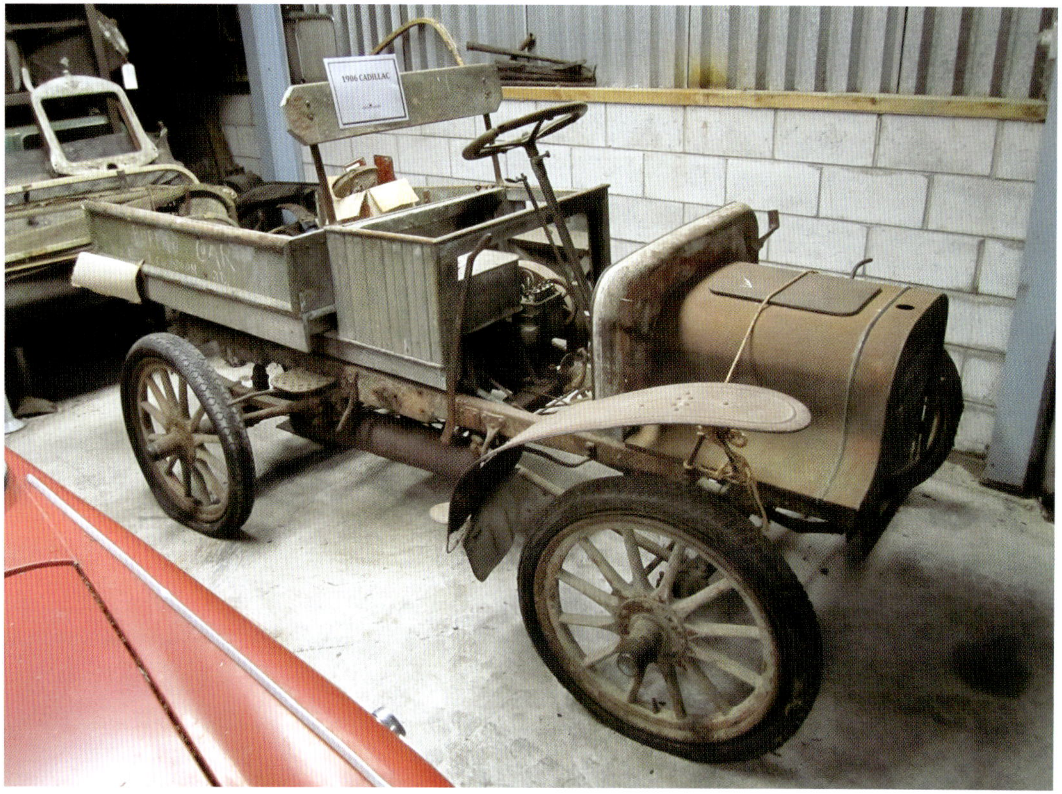
1906 CADILLAC

1906
GOBRON-BRILLE

HENRY FORD

BURKE ST
SUNOCO
RACE FUELS
Bud
SPEED LIMIT
35
MILES
BH1172

It is while on a road trip to Christchurch with a buddy of mine, there to race his '69 Mustang at Ruapuna, that I first get to see Steve's awesome cave, out the back of Burkes Metalworks. Like the guy I am travelling with, Steve also races a '69 Mustang, and in fact will be racing against my buddy the weekend we are there. Thanks to Jason Burke, director of Burkes Metalworks, we get to take a tour of the workshops, viewing the vast number of projects these guys are working on, which include everything from vintage cars to a Holden Monaro. The level of workmanship is really impressive, but that should be expected, as Gus Burke, Jason's dad and the founder of this company, is something of a metal craftsman and his high standards have been passed down to Jason.

The workshop is impressive, but damn, it's also pretty noisy! When it gets too much, Jason takes us out to meet Steve (Jason's cousin), a motor vehicle painter — and that's when I get to see their amazing shop/bar/storage area/vehicle assembly area/automobilia display area. As general manager, Steve now runs the business side of Burkes and this is where he does most of his work, away from the hustle and bustle, and noise of the main workshop. And Jason also often comes here to reassemble cars that the team has worked on.

This is a truly incredible place. I am immediately taken by the bar, with its bar stools made from bent tubing and other materials found around the workshop, and modified to suit, and even a seat created out of a thick tree trunk. The bar-tops sit on old wooden barrels, while the entire floor in the bar area is carpeted with bottle tops. This is definitely a bloke's place. Corrugated iron lines the walls around the bar, covered by old licence plates and photos.

Cars come and go in this area, but one that remains a constant is Steve's own '69 Mustang fastback race car. This car has been built to replicate Allan Moffat's famous '69 Coca-Cola Mustang that was raced to great success in Australia and New Zealand from 1969 to 1975. Additionally, Burkes is currently working on its own heavily modified Camaro, designed by Jason, which will become a showcase for the business. Jason has spent time in the United States, working as a fabricator on various show cars there, and has already amassed an impressive list of awards for his efforts. The Camaro is far from finished but is already an incredible piece of work, with every exterior panel having been heavily modified and manipulated to the point where nothing is original. The car is now lower and wider than the standard version, and yet it's still instantly recognizable as a 1970 Camaro.

I've got no doubts whatsoever that this place really comes to life in the evenings and has become something of a social hub for local enthusiasts, who do their best to empty the large stockpile of beer in the fridge.

SPEED LIMIT
35
MILES
HIGH-FLOW

TEXACO
Gulf

C/- Jim Day
New Zealand

TEXACO
Gulf
TEXACO

MARYLAND
DNS 725
404F557
PMW 732
X 27895
ML-220
PZZ-463
42070
264 JKG

Budweiser
Coors Light

Green Mountain State
SMIRNOFF
ICE

Lite
ON TAP
BURKE ST
BURKES METALWORKS RACING

Lite
ON TAP
Silver Bullet

SHINE
SHINE
SPEED SHOP
POLLY

Marlboro
BUD LIGHT
DIXIE
TEXACO
Extreme Rides
SKOPE
2009

RACE FUELS
BURKE S
CQJ232

THE RUSH FAMILY

It is John at Southward Car Museum (see page 152) who suggests I contact Terry Rush. John has known Terry for years, and gives me a brief overview of Terry's collection — which goes something like, 'He's got several Formula 5000 cars, and a bunch of Morris Minors.' I know that Terry has some F5000 cars in his collection, as he and son Tim exercise them regularly as part of the Trans Tasman Revival Series. But I am curious as to how someone with a passion for thundering F5000 race cars can also have an interest in Morris Minors, a model about as far removed from a Formula 5000 as it's possible to be. Terry is more than happy for me to include him in the book, but is out of the country at the time I want to visit. However, his son Tim is pleased to show me around.

The amazing thing in putting this book together is that no matter what I think I'm going to see, I'm always wrong. Here I am thinking I'm about to view a small collection of F5000 cars and some Morris Minors, and Tim takes me into what can only be described as a private museum. And its contents are vastly greater, more varied and more interesting than I could have imagined. We enter a large, recently built but quite characterful barn, lined with tin on an impressive timber frame. In a modest-sized room are a few chairs and couches, and an almighty collection of old motoring and motor-racing magazines and books. I'm quite happy to spend the next hour thumbing through these, but I sense that Tim wants me to move into the next section of the barn, so I follow him through. And it's at this point that my jaw really hits the floor. 'I love watching people's faces when they first walk in here,' announces Tim. I'm not surprised; this collection is incredibly impressive.

I do a quick visual scan around the building and notice all manner of machinery, from the promised Morris Minors (it turns out the Morris Minors are Tim's passion, and he has owned several since he was a teenager) through to large vintage commercial vehicles, and cabinets full of model cars, automobilia and memorabilia. The place is predominantly motoring-related, but this family holds a deep sense of pride in history in general.

My love of motor racing was the main motivation for wanting to see this collection, and these guys have some really impressive racing machines here, including a Cooper 500, a Brabham BT4 formerly raced by both Jack Brabham and Denny Hulme, a Lola T142 Formula 5000 formerly raced by Swede Ulf Norinder, David Oxton's beautiful Begg FM4 Formula 5000, and a further two F5000 cars, these being the McLaren M22 (the last F5000 car built by McLaren) and the massive McRae GM3/GM9. This car began life as an F5000, with wild clear-Perspex top

McLaren M22
Details
History
McLAREN CARS
20
Mc LAREN CARS
BONNEY'S
SPECIALISED TRANSPORT
Mobil 1

cowl, in which Graham McRae won the 1978 Australian Grand Prix, and which was then rebuilt into a Can-Am sports car with magnificent aluminium bodywork crafted by Steve Roberts, at which point it was assigned the designation GM9.

Terry has been a motorsport enthusiast all his life, having competed when he was younger, and was one of the small group of local resident racers responsible for the creation of the Manfeild race track on the outskirts of Feilding, which first opened its gates in 1973. Terry is also Manfeild Club chairman. Several interesting photos are displayed in the Rush collection of the Manfeild grounds when the design and construction of this track took place. So it makes sense that the Rush family collection has such a strong motorsport theme.

Beyond the race cars I am struck by a neatly turned out mock petrol station forecourt, in which is parked a Ford Anglia. Three commercial vehicles are lined up next to each other, the last being a beautiful vintage fire engine. The motor, a glorious and monstrous Seagrave V12, has been removed for refurbishment and is mounted on a stand in the next room.

I'm impressed by what the Rush family has achieved here. They've saved some important race cars from leaving New Zealand shores, and they've preserved pieces of local history that otherwise would have been scrapped and lost forever. The Rush family collection is open by private viewing, and is located in Feilding, the home of 'Magic Manfeild'.

WIN TOTAL

GARAGE
CHAMPION
SPARK PLUGS
CALTEX
PETROL

Shell SPORT
STP
Benelli
162

Clear-Perspex McRae GM3 top cowl hangs on the Rush family's wall.

TONY F

'The great thing about classic cars is that there is always somewhere to use them,' Tony explains to me as we're walking through his vast and varied collection. 'There are clubs for just about every classic car ever made, and there are always events being held.' That's true for anyone who owns a classic car — but Tony has a whole fleet of them. Rather than sticking to a single theme, as many enthusiasts do, he tends to buy cars he likes, regardless of how well they fit with the rest of the collection. And so his garages feature everything from a late-model Ferrari 348 through to a 1965 Mustang.

Tony has two large garages. The first, which I find the most interesting, houses the '65 Mustang coupé, a genuine 1970 Boss 302 Mustang, a GTR Torana which was his first race car, a Capri race car which replaced the Torana as his track gun, a VL Walkinshaw replica Commodore which replaced the Capri, plus the Ferrari. The walls and ceiling of the garage are completely lined with the hundreds of posters Tony has collected over many years, and is far more interesting than any paint job. 'You need to install a couch in here, Tony, so you can lie here and take in all the ceiling art,' I suggest.

Next door, in the new tin barn, he has a third-generation Ford Mustang, a stunning Ford Thunderbird, formerly owned by Marc Ellis, a rare Ford Sierra Cosworth RS500, and an equally rare E49 Valiant Charger. As I said, the collection is varied; but all the cars get used, and are enjoyed in their own way and for different occasions. The new barn is not yet fully lined with the laminated poster treatment that decorates the older garage, but Tony has made a start, working his way down one of the walls.

I'm particularly excited by the Sierra Cosworth, as I fell in love with these wild turbo machines as a teenager in the 1980s when they were first released. With a top speed of 155 mph, they were considered quite insane at the time, given that they were, essentially, a four-seat family hatchback. Joyriders in the UK loved them, and that pushed insurance premiums through the roof. Tony's example is a rare RS500 model, which Ford produced to further homologate additional upgrades to the standard Sierra RS Cosworth, such as larger turbo and extra spoilers. Only 500 of these (hence the name) were made. Another rare beast is the E49 Charger. As was typical of some dealerships in Australia, they'd personalize their performance cars to make them stand out from those offered by other dealers. Tony's E49 was fitted at the dealership with Pacer hood stripes.

So, it being true that there is always somewhere to use a classic car, I expect Tony's weekends are fairly busy.

HOLDEN
16
Castrol
Gladstone
CYCLES
691
AUSTRALIAN
AIRLINES
Telecom Mobiles
PARKROYAL
Dulux
Autocolour
TOOHEYS 1000
Allan Grice
Win Percy
Holden's Engine Company

dstone
CLES

FORDE

34

SPEED
LIMIT
NONE
RESERVED
PARKING
CHARGER
HOLDEN
Castrol
Dulux
Autocolour
DUNLOP
TOW
Telecom Mobiles

MUSTANG GT
83GTHØ

YA1963

MOTOR
RACING
SERIES

BIG BROTHER
HOLDING CO.
JANIS JOPLIN
"HOLIDAY" WEEKEND CONCERT
SUNDAY
NOV. 10th
WESTCHESTER COUNTY CENTER
WHITE PLAINS, NEW YORK
BROOKLYN ROCK
BROOKLYN, NEW YORK
THE BYRDS
IRON BUTTERFLY
BIG BROTHER
YOUNGBLOODS
COUNTRY JOE
GRATEFUL DEAD
JEFFERSON AIRPLANE
CITY PARK STADIUM
THURS AUGUST 1, 1968
CONCERT WEST PRESENTS
JIMI
"PURPLE HAZE"
"WILD THING"
HENDRIX
EXPERIENCE
NEW YEAR'S EVE
GRATEFUL DEAD
BLUES BROTHERS
N.R.P.S.
Breakfast Served at Dawn
WINTERLAN
DEC. 31 · 1978
YW4414

Incredible Lister Chevrolet with Costin body. This was the first Costin-bodied Lister, and the first with Chevrolet V8 power.

TONY G

Back around 1990, when I was a teenager, I was visiting a race event at Manfeild in which there was a big field of Formula Ford racers. In among them all one car stood out, as much as anything for its colour scheme, which was a bold blue very similar to the Leyton House March Formula 1 cars of the era. This car was driven by a bloke called Tony Garmey. By complete coincidence, a few years later when I was doing my OE in London, I worked with a fellow called Mark Garmey, who turned out to be Tony's younger brother and who filled me in on Tony's activities. By this stage, Tony was living and working in the US, race-preparing and maintaining historic race cars for Vintage Racing Motors, where Bruce McCaw was and is a major client. McCaw, as some readers will know, eventually started the PacWest Racing IndyCar and Indy Lights team, in which Scott Dixon got his big break in the US. Tony and I eventually came into contact after 20 years of knocking around in similar circles after Tony joined the historic motorsport website and forum I run, theroaringseason.com.

Tony actually started out racing in historics, with his dad's Cooper 500 and a self-built Mini Cooper, and despite various forays in and out of Formula Ford, including races at Hockenheim, at Le Mans and Midget racing in the US, he kept coming back to historics. In the late 1990s he began working for Pat Hart in Redmond, Washington. Pat's massive collection of historic road and race cars included numerous Ferraris and a 1957 Fiat Ferrari race car transporter. As Tony describes it, 'I was mechanic/travel agent/truck driver/race driver.' Essentially, Tony worked on a large car collection, containing 54 exotic machines, and then got to drive them on weekends! Not a bad way to earn a living.

In 2001 Tony set up Horizon Racing and Performance, in Maple Valley, Washington, offering an array of services mostly for historic race car owners, providing everything from driver training to transportation of cars to and from events, to trackside support, plus a full complement of restoration, rebuild, and refurbishment and fabrication services. His list of clients has continued to grow, and he gets to work on and race some amazing and exotic machines. Pat Hart died in 2001, but Tony still works on some of the cars from the Hart family collection.

Unlike in New Zealand, in the US many owners of historic race cars, especially those at the high end, prefer to have other, more experienced peddlers drive their cars for them. Tony can thus be seen racing all types of machinery, from a monster McLaren M8C Can-Am car through to the one-off prototype Triumph

TR250K, a futuristic 'Speed Racer'-style machine designed by Pete Brock, better known as the designer of the Daytona Cobra coupés built by Carroll Shelby's race team. This car competed at the Sebring 12-hour classic in 1968. Other cars in Tony's workshop include a Bobsy SR3, a Chevron B17B, plus a Lister Costin Chevy, which was the Costin prototype, and the first Lister to leave the factory fitted with Chevrolet V8 power, rather than Jaguar power, this particular example also being fitted with Hilborn mechanical fuel injection. He also has a Devin SS and a Devin TR, a Peyote, and a Ferrari 275 GTB/4 'which came to me on a billy cart and in 19 boxes of milk crates, and is one of 15 made', according to Tony. There's also a Ford GT40 built by Ray Mallock, the McLaren M4B, a Ferrari 250 GT Fantuzzi, and a Boss 302 Trans-Am Mustang (ex Parnelli Jones). The Garry Pederson New Zealand-built sports car, the Gemco, is arriving soon for restoration, among others.

Even Tony's workshop is a salubrious historic building, which perfectly suits the machines sitting between the chunky columns that are part of the building's architecture. '"The barn", as we call it, is 6000 square foot and where we do most of our work. I have 1400 square foot at our home where we do most of our chassis work and major fab.' Sounds ideal! I can't imagine that Tony is in too much of a hurry to move back to New Zealand any time soon.

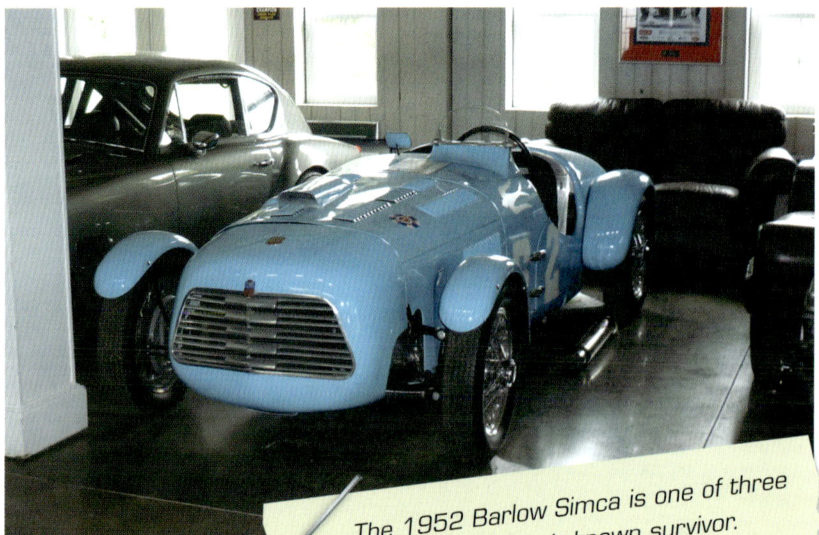

The 1952 Barlow Simca is one of three made, and the only known survivor.

Ferrari 250GT Fantuzzi.

Wild Triumph 250K.

222

GARMEY
19

Tony at speed in a McLaren M8C.

ACKNOWLEDGEMENTS

This book would never have seen the light of day without the help, support and enthusiasm of those who got behind it. To create a book such as this, profiling private garages and collections, only word of mouth will work. To that end, I'd like to thank John Bellamore, Hayden Beissel, Pete Jacobs, John Armitstead, Wally Willmott, Jeremy Were, Rhys Nolan, Tim Rush, Garry Price and Bryan Morris, for recommending people of interest and then, in some cases, paving the way to allow me access.

I'd also like to thank Todd at *NZV8* magazine, for supplying a good portion of the photos for the chapters on George and all the photos for Steve. Although I was able to visit both garages, in the case of George I could only photograph the tidier parts of his garage, but Todd had been through a few months earlier for a photoshoot and provided the photos for the remaining areas. In the case of Steve at Burkes Metalworks a cancelled flight into Christchurch scuppered my plans, but fortunately Todd came to the rescue once more.

Martin Rudow kindly supplied the photos for Tony Garmey's workshop in Maple Valley, Washington. Martin is the editor of *Pacific Northwest Racing*.

I'd also like to thank HarperCollins Publishers for their continued enthusiasm and support, and in particular Bill Honeybone who always goes in to bat for me, pushing to get the green light on many of my ideas. HarperCollins have a dedicated and hard-working team which produces some stunning books, and they're a joy to work with.

To all the individuals featured in this book who welcomed me into their homes and their garages and opened them up for fellow enthusiasts to enjoy and be inspired by, a big thanks.

I'd like to thank my parents, Marianne and Glenn, for providing me a place to stay when passing through Palmerston North, and healthy meals that offset the energy drinks and mince pies that are my usual staple diet when on the road.

Finally, I'd like to thank my wonderful partner Helen, for looking after our idiotic dogs, keeping everything held together in my absence and for being my personal assistant (albeit with very minor complaining) while I'm on the road, sorting motels and hotels for me and finding the best prices on everything from accommodation to flights and rental cars while juggling a very busy career. I really do appreciate it.

ABOUT THE AUTHOR

Steve Holmes has been writing for specialist car magazines for more than 10 years. He started out doing the promotional work for Te Marua Speedway in Upper Hutt for a couple of seasons, before graduating to write predominantly race car and New Zealand motorsport history pieces (the latter a lifelong passion) for various New Zealand and Australian magazines. Steve's first book, *The Kiwi Hot Rodder's Guide to Life*, was published by HarperCollins in 2011, with his second book, *The Kiwi Ute Driver's Guide to Life*, following a year later.

Steve makes a living as a graphic designer (www.monsterracewear.co.nz), creating mostly custom T-shirt artwork and concept cars for various customers, as well as motoring-related websites. His enthusiasm for motorsport history has also seen him create an online international historic motorsport website and forum called The Roaring Season (www.theroaringseason.com), which has enjoyed rapid growth since its inception and been responsible for a great number of wonderful stories and old racing photographs being made public. A large number of racers and team members from the past, all around the world, have become members and regular contributors.

Steve lives on a one-acre lifestyle block in the Wairarapa with his partner Helen and their two dogs and one cat.

enquiries@monsterracewear.co.nz